# Chapter One

Couponing. The basics and how to make it easy.

One thing I want you to realize is the first time you coupon, you will save money. However since you will not have all the materials needed to effectively save massive amounts of money yet, you will be saving more within a month or so. This is where a lot of people get discouraged at. It is hard to understand when you see others on television or even your friends tell you how much they are saving and then you go to the store and save $9.00. You tried putting everything together and you only saved $9.00. It will not seem like it's worth the trouble until you get all your materials together. The longer you do it, the more you will end up saving. Remember when you are starting out, you will not have all the materials needed to save a lot of money, you will collect these things as you go along. The more materials you have the more you will save. I will give you several places to go for coupons to help get you started so you do not get frustrated in the beginning.

The goal of couponing is to get the lowest price available on any given product. I will teach you how to maximize your saving and how to know when is the best time to make a purchase.

COUPONS

Ask yourself, "Do you really know what coupons are?" Coupons are incentives to entice the consumer to buy a company's product. Coupons are used like money since they help pay or actually pay for an item.

I'm sure you all know what a coupon is but did you know all manufactured coupons start with a 5 or a 9. If they start with a 9 they WILL DOUBLE. If they start with a 5 they are not suppose to double but that is up to the store you shop at and their store policy. For example, Publix will honor a manufacture's coupon which starts with a 5, for the full amount of the coupon and it is their policy to double coupons up to .50 no matter what the coupon starts with. This is one of their incentives to get you to come to their store and buy their products.

Always follow the wording on the coupon. If the coupon states 4 like items in one transaction, please do not try to get 6 like items in one transaction using coupons. The only time you should do this willingly is when you already know the store's policy and they allow overage. Publix and Bi-Lo, for instance, usually allow up to 10 like items with coupons in the same transaction. This is depending on your store. It is always best to check with customer service to verify what your particular store will allow. You can do one better and ask for a print out of their coupon policy. You should be able to get one at the store's customer service. If the store does not have their policy on hand, go online to their website and print one off. If there is no link simply request one to be mailed to you.

When a coupon states 4 like items in one transaction, what they are saying is you can buy 4 of the same items such as Pepsi 2 liters and use 4 coupons in one transaction. That does not stop you from buying more than 4 of the same item. You can buy 10 if your store will allow it, however, you can only use 4 coupons in that transaction.

Coupons are going to the GS1 DataBar Coupon format. This will provide manufacturers more options for purchase requirements and values and make it possible to code more complex offers. It will also enable the coupon to be validated at checkout for the manufacturer's intended purchase. For example, if the coupon is for Crest toothpaste it cannot be used for Crest mouthwash. It should reduce mis-redemption. The GSI DataBar Coupon format will also help retailers with scanning accuracy. More specific coding and fewer human readable elements should help reduce mis-redemption, while minimizing the amount of "hard-to-handle" coupons. GSI will also help retailers be able to code chain-specific promotions.

Mis-redemption is one of the reasons some stores have a hard time accepting coupons and makes it harder on the honest coupon-er. A manufacturer will put out coupons to help sell a certain product such as yogurt, however, if the store is accepting coupons for the wrong brand of yogurt then they are taking the chance of not getting their money back. When this happens on a consistent bases the store may put a freeze on accepting coupons or they may tighten the belt (so to say) on which coupons they may accept. For instance, the store may start only accepting coupons out of the Sunday paper and no longer accept printable coupons. There are people who do not get the Sunday paper but only use printable coupons. That would make it difficult for these people to save money without purchasing the Sunday paper.

Coupons are not a way for a store to get rid of expired products. Coupons do not cause a store to lose money if used correctly. When a store collects a coupon and sends it into the manufacturer, they are paid for the face value of that coupon plus usually about .08. This information is clearly found on the coupon. If your store doubles coupons, then they may be out the additional doubled amount. However trust me when I say that stores do not pay anywhere close to what they charge for the products they sell. Stores have a huge mark up. They are in the business to make money and if doubling a coupon makes them lose money, they simply would not allow it.

The different types of coupons.

Manufactured Coupons

Manufactured coupons come straight from the manufacturer such as Yoplait, General Mills, Tampax, Lipton etc. They can usually be found in inserts from the Sunday paper. Some products will have manufactured coupons on the product you are about to purchase.  These coupons are call pullies.  Usually pullies are not as good as the ones from the paper, however, their expiration dates are longer.  These coupons are put on by the vendor of the product and are not "owned" by the store they are in.  If you think this would be a good coupon to use at a later date, you can pull them from the item.  These coupons would be good to use when an item goes on sale and your coupon from the Sunday paper or printable has expired.  Now, I personally do not pull any more than two from the same item.  I feel this is fair to the other consumers.  You can also find them on the grocery alleys, in boxes.  These boxes are called tear pads. The tear pad boxes can sometimes be easily spotted with a red blinking light.  Once you pull the manufactured coupon from the box it will slide another one out.  If you are looking for another one to slide out you may have to wait a minute or two.  It appears their timer gets longer once the second one is pulled out.  Each of these coupons will come with a barcode that will start with a 5 or a 9.  They will also have an expiration date.

Printables

These coupons are printed online from a printer. You must install a coupon printer software in order to print coupons online. The first time you try to print a coupon you should be prompted to download the program into your computer. Special note: When printing your first online printable coupon, print a coupon you really do not want. Occasionally when you first install the online coupon software you will have to restart your computer. When this happens, your coupons usually gets lost. You can normally go to a manufacturer's website and look for coupons or promotions which can be printed. When the manufacturer is offering printable coupons or promotions you simply print them off. One thing to remember is you can only print 2 per ISP address. The simplest way to do this is to print the coupon the first time. Once the coupon has printed, hit the back button. You will be prompted to resend the information, select yes and it will print once again. It should not print after this process as companies which put out the printable coupons have a program in place to stop the user from printing more than two. One notable thing, if the coupon is in a PDF file you should be able to save the coupon to your computer and print it as many times as you like. Printable coupons come in the form of store or manufactured coupons. Keep in mind they will have an expiration date.

Note on ISP addresses. Each computer has an ISP address and usually each computer in one household has the same ISP address. If you want to print more than two printable coupons you will need to go to a different location to get another ISP address.

Electronic or E-coupons

Electronic coupons can be loaded onto your store loyalty rewards card such as Bi-lo, Kroger or Publix. Bi-lo's store loyalty reward card is call "fuel perks". Typically you can load e-coupons onto your card through the internet. To load your loyalty reward card, go to the store's website. Register for their site. Locate the area to register your loyalty reward card. In the area provided input the loyalty number. Once you have registered your card, go to the section labeled "ecoupons". Then pick the coupons you would like to add, click on the coupon and the system should load them onto your card.

Once your e-coupon is loaded, when you have purchased a product which is loaded on your card, the amount of the coupon will come off your bill and will automatically come off of your store rewards card. There is no thinking involved, when e-coupons expire; they will automatically come off of your store rewards card. Typically I will load all loyalty cards at the beginning of the month when new coupons come out. There is a limit to how many companies will allow to be loaded so getting them loaded as quickly as possibly will maximize your savings.

## Competitors coupon

A competitor's coupon is a coupon which does not belong to the current store you are shopping at. Competitor coupons act just like a store coupon but they do not come from that particular store. Many stores will accept competitor coupons within a certain mile range of their store. Always check with your customer service to verify which competitor store coupons they accept before heading to the checkout line. This will save you any embarrassment.

## Store coupons

A store coupon is exactly as it sounds. It comes from the store you are shopping at. Many stores will have them at customer service. Another place to find store coupons is on the store isles, usually before an item goes on sale. They are placed next to an item, by the store, to entice the consumer to buy that product. In many cases, that item will go on sale. When it goes on sale, you can now use the store coupon (as long as it has not expired) and if you have a manufactured coupon and your store allows stacking, chances are you can get the item for next to nothing. Rule of thumb, these are good to hold on to. Typically, store coupons will not have a barcode and will not double. The fun thing about a store coupon is many stores will let you stack them.

What is stacking?

Stacking is the practice of compiling multiple coupons for one item. This does not mean you can use multiple manufactured coupons for one item. Companies which allow stacking will accept a store coupon (or competitor's store coupon) and one manufactured coupon on the same item. In essence, you are using two different coupons for the same item. If this doesn't already sound good, what would you say if I told you stacking can be used on a sale item also?

For example:  If your store has Total cereal on sale.  The original cost was 3.99 and now it is on sale for $2.50.  You have a store coupon for $1.00 off one (either from their store or a competitors store) and you have a manufacture coupon for .50 off (which may double to $1.00).  Now the $3.99 box of cereal is either .50 or $1.00, if the coupon has doubled.  This is when you buy enough cereal to last your family until it goes on sale again.

Sales:

Sales rotate in cycles.  If you find an item on sale this week, chances are they will not be on sale next week in the same store.  General Mills cereal may be on sale this week and next week Post cereal will be on sale.  The object is to buy enough of the sale item to last you until the next sale comes around.  Sales priced items typically come in 6 to 8 week cycles.  This means you will get the lowest price available during this time.  Compile the sale of an item with coupons and the item is now at its lowest price available.  With the different sales and coupons it is up to you to know how many to buy of one product.  For example, I have 6 children making my household a total of 8 people. When I find whole wheat pasta on sale, I know I need to buy 2 boxes for each meal that I plan. I plan for at least one pasta night a week for a total of 2 boxes a week. I need 2 boxes a week for 8 weeks for a total of 16 boxes. This is only typical for a family this size. You may only need one box a week for 8 weeks. The point is to buy enough to last you until the sale comes around again. One of my biggest pet peeves is when I use to run out of an item and would have to buy it only with a coupon and not have it on sale. That's just like throwing money in the trash can and not in the bank.

Example: French's mustard starts off at $1.48. You find a store that offers BOGO (Buy One Get One Free). If that store put a price on each of the two bottles of mustard, that mustard becomes .74 each. Another way to look at it is each item is 50% off. If you have two coupons for .50 off one bottle of French's mustard and it doubles to a $1.00 then you just made a .26 profit off mustard. Usually what happens is the store will enter the coupon manually and will makes the item free. For instance, instead of taking the $1.00 off they will manually put in the coupon for .74 (the sale price) making the item free.  If you are lucky to have a store that will give you the full amount of each coupon, then overage will be taken off of your final bill.  So if you purchased 5 French's mustard and the store gives you the overage of .26, you now have $1.30 towards your overall bill.  What does this mean for you?  The cashier will ring up your total and will credit your grocery bill with the regular coupons which does not have overages.  Then if your out of pocket, after coupons, was $5.00, the store will take the additional $1.30 off and your new out of pocket will be a total of $3.70.

Seasonal Sale:

Seasonal sales are items that typically go on sale around a particular holiday or season of the year.  For example, around Super Bowl Sunday, you would likely find chips, salsa and soda on sale for all the Super Bowl parties.  Another example would be cake mixes going on sale around Christmas or Thanksgiving.  These items also go on sale during the rest of the year but typically you will see them on sale during these times also.

I am not a big fan of Walmart because they advertise having lowest prices which means they are not going to go any lower.

They do not have "sales" on food products, they simply state a new lower price. The lower price they are referring to may be .20 or .02. They accept manufactured coupons from the Sunday paper at face value. So if a coupon is .50, Wal-Mart will not double, it simply takes .50 off the product. Let me tell you what I do like about Wal-Mart. Wal-Mart will price match from any local store in the area. Many Wal-Mart stores are keeping binders around the register with local sale ads. I would suggest bring your own. Without proof you will not get the price match. Price match means taking an advertised price from another store and sell it to you for the same amount. It would be as if you are at the competitors store and bought the item except you didn't have to spend the gas to actually go there.

For example: Save A Lot had Butter Ball Turkey Bacon on sale 10 for $10.00 or $1.00 a pack. Since I don't shop at Save A Lot, I took the ad from the Sunday paper with me to Wal-Mart. I found a .55 off one package of butter Ball Turkey Bacon manufactured coupon which made my bacon .45. Wal-Mart doesn't double coupons, they do not take competitors coupons, they do not have store coupons and they have given me enough grief with printable coupons that I will not use them there, but they will price match. The best time to price match at Wal-Mart is with a high value coupon. For example, Finish dishwasher detergent tablets are usually a descent price at Wal-Mart without a sale. When the manufacturer puts out a coupon for $1.25 off or more, this would be the time to use it. The $1.25 off coupon will not double making the better price at Wal-Mart if your regular store does not have the item on sale.

Coupon Courtesy:

Many store policies will only take 10 of the same like coupon for an item. So if you have 11 mustards you should know that most places will only take 10 manufactured coupons for the mustards you are buying. That doesn't mean they won't take them but it puts the cashier in a position they shouldn't be put in. You can always go to another store or make another trip the next day. This also does not mean you cannot buy the 11 containers of mustards, it only means you can only use 10 coupons for them. For example, if the mustard is on sale for .74 each and you have a .50 off coupon, you will pay .24 off 10 of the mustards, now on the 11$^{th}$ one, you will pay the sale price of .74. Some stores will limit the quantity you can purchase in one transaction.  Always, remember to check with customer service prior, if you are unsure.

If you have a Bilo fuel perks card and you want to get the mustard deal multiple times, you can.  However, you can only use the card 4 times in one day, for the same product.  Anything over 4 times a day, the system will flag your card and a manager has the right to either override the system or cancel the transaction completely.

Expired coupons:

Some stores will allow you to use expired coupons up to a few days and some even up to a week after the coupon has expired.  The reasons some companies will allow this practices is one, it encourages the consumer to come to their store, and two, many will not mail their coupons for reimbursements until the end of the month.  This will allow them to still receive their money, so they have not lost anything.

With the new GSI DateBar the practice of using expired coupons may become obsolete.  You may have many expired coupons simply because they are for things you will not use.  So you may be asking yourself, "What do I do with the expired coupons?" A great practice is to pay it forward. The military service members and their families serving our country overseas are allowed to use coupons up to 6 months after they have expired at their commissary. You can go online and find an overseas military base to donate them to or you can adopt a military family and send your expired coupons to them. Go to this website: http://www.ocpnet.org/Base%20List/BaseList1.htm. You do not have to tell them you are adopting them, just put the coupons in a priority envelope and stick them in the mail. Even though there is an oversea address you will not be required to pay overseas shipping. The military's mail goes to a centrally located post office in the states before going overseas. You are simply paying for it to go there. Know they are very thankful for all the help they can get.

Shelf clearing:

Shelf clearing is the act of taking the entire same product off the shelf. This does not mean taking the last two of an item. This means there are 20 left of one product and you purchase 10 in one transaction and turn around and make an additional transaction with the last 10, not leaving any for other customers. Shelf clearing is not a good practice and it makes people mad. I, typically, will get a few of my items at the beginning of a sale and the rest at the end or last day of the sale. The best part about getting them at the end of a sale is (as long as you are not using coupons that are expiring) if a store has run out of a product, they will give you a rain check at customer service for up to 10 items. Some rain checks will expire in 30 days but there are many that do not expire. The point is if you don't have all your coupons together you will have the opportunity to do so now.

Where do you get coupons?

Coupons can be printed offline through various websites. You can go straight to the manufactuer's website to see if they have printable coupons. Remember 2 per ISP address unless it has been formatted into a PDF file. This does not mean per computer so please don't get confused.

There are several websites where you can print coupons from. There are even websites you can make money by printing them. This will be discussed in a later chapter. When going to manufacture's websites, go to the printable section and look around to find the products you are interested in. Many manufactured websites list their printable coupons around the beginning of the month and there is a limited quantity allowed to be printed. I would suggest on the first day of the month, print any coupons you would normally use and print off coupons for things you would like to try. If an item you would like to try goes on sale, you can pair it with a coupon to maximize your savings. If you print a coupon you do not use simply throw it away when it expires. Do not worry about the paper and ink, I have dedicated a section of this book to show you have to make money rather than waste money with printing coupons.

The Sunday Paper:

If you do not subscribe to the Sunday paper I would recommend it if they come with coupons in them. Typically you can get an introductory price for at least 6 months. The introductory offer occasionally offers a percentage off of an automatic payment plan plus free delivery. Once the introductory offer has expired you can decide where to drive to pick up your papers or continue with the service. Additionally, if you are set up for automatic payments, the introductory offer will continue without interruptions and without an additional delivery fee. Verify there is no delivery fee after the introductory offer before signing up. If there is an additional delivery fee, it is now up to you whether or not you want to continue the service. Ask the questions before you make your decision.

One nice thing about the Sunday paper coupons is freebies. Many times when a manufacturer makes a new product they put a free coupon in the Sunday paper so you will try the product. Another fun thing is finding rebate forms in the coupon section of the Sunday paper. These come in handy when you purchase an item for $2.99 and have a coupon for a $1.00 off. You pay $1.99 out of pocket, submit the proper paperwork and receive full price for the item in the mail. These are called money makers.

The Sunday paper comes with inserts. The inserts contains the coupons. The names of the inserts you should be looking for are:

Red Plum

Smart Source

Proctor & Gamble

Occasionally manufactures will have special inserts from their companies such as General Mills. There is no guarantee which coupons will be in which papers. Usually, the Sunday closest to the next month is when Proctor & Gamble's insert will come out. This is usually the only time Proctor & Gamble puts out coupons. I tend to purchase extra papers when Proctor & Gamble is included, knowing they only come out once a month. There are several websites, listed later in the book, to verify which inserts should be in the Sunday paper. A general rule is that holiday weekends usually will not have inserts.

You can sign up and register at the inserts websites. For example, go to www.smartsource.com and print off coupons. Proctor & Gamble generally does not have many printable coupons. However, on their website, you can sign up to get their additional booklets. The booklets are mailed out periodically and have great coupons in them.

Purchasing coupons:

A great way to get started is to just purchase coupons online. This will allow you the opportunity to get past issues of inserts so you are ready to make your list and start saving. Past issues of inserts will be more than the initial cost of a Sunday paper; this is how people make their money. Don't worry, the amount you pay for the insert will be far less than the savings you will receive, especially for those that double. Many papers will have anywhere from $200.00 to 500.00 in coupons (before doubling). If you had to pay $5.00 for the inserts of a Sunday paper, you have still made money when using the coupons.

Ebay:

I like ordering from Ebay when I know I am going to get a product FREE or Make Money off of the transaction. Sellers on Ebay will advertise coupons in many different denominations. I look for batches with more quantity at the lowest selling price. Why this works best for me? Say mustard is on sale at .74 each and a batch of 20 mustard coupons for .50 off one bottle is selling for 1.49. Knowing that store I shop at will double this coupon to a $1.00, I know I am making .26 off each bottle or $5.20 for all 20 bottles. I will now purchase those hard to get deals on items such as meat. I do not think I will use 20 bottles of mustard before they go bad, instead I will take out the amount my household will need and I will donate the rest to a local food bank or a church with a food bank. Coupons read "Void if altered, copied, sold, purchased, transferred, exchanged or where prohibited or restricted by law." For this purpose Ebay does not allow the actually selling of coupons. Per Ebay's policy sellers are allow to auction off the time it takes to collect, cut and ship coupons. Although this sounds confusing, you actually receive the coupons, the sellers are just not allow to say they are selling them.

The Coupon Clippers:

The Coupon Clipper's company is simple and easy to use. Register for an account. Once you have registered, log in, search for the coupon you want and if they have it in stock, it will show up. Their minimum purchase is $3.96 and this will include a .46 shipping fee (for the stamp) and .50 administrative fee. The coupons will range from .08 to .25 depending on the value. Usually a FREE product is going to be on the higher end. The regular coupons are between .08-.12. What I like best is you can make your grocery list from the internet, order only what is needed and usually get the coupons within a few days. They have a tally saying when they will ship new orders on the website so you do not need to wonder. When considering this company keep in mind they are based out of Florida. Later you will learn how to get your shopping list together prior to the sale. Once you get your list together, order your coupons and wait for them to come in.

Coupon Swaps:

These can usually be found in newspapers or local events (groups) such as churches. Some websites which promote coupons also have coupon swaps.

The Dreaded Binder:

Have you ever seen someone walking around the store with a huge binder full of papers hanging out everywhere, or seen someone with a binder talking to themselves, asking "Was it in box foods or breakfast foods?" then frantically looking for that one coupon? Here is what you will need to ensure you are not that person with the big binder.

This is what you will need to make your couponing successful and less stressful.

Computer

New Email Address

Printer (and paper...not to worry, I will show you in later chapters how to get paper and ink for next to nothing)

Newspapers

File Folders

Computer:

Yes, you will need a computer. The computer will not only cut down on the time it takes to make your shopping list, it will also enable you to find the deals and make the process easier. I am all about making this easy.

New Email:

The purpose for a separate email is to keep your personal emails and your couponing or spam emails separate. It's so frustrating trying to find an email a friend said they sent you in your inbox that is full of spam. The easiest way to set up a new email is to use your current email but with a different provider. Using the same email but with a different provider will make it easier to remember. So if your current email is: johnsmith@gmail.com you may consider using johnsmith@yahoo.com with the same password. You will be registering with different sites as you come across them. You register for these sites because they will send you emails with coupons in them that you otherwise may not be able to find.

Printer:

When you get coupons in emails you will need to be able to print them, which means you will need a printer...if you don't already have one.

Special Note: Unless you absolutely have to have a specific coupon, print in increments of three. Three coupons will print on one page. This will help save on paper. Here is another reason to print in increments of three. Let's say you paid full price (you won't but let's say you did) for a case of paper at $50.00. Each case has 5000 sheets of paper in them, making each sheet .01 each. If you print 3 usable coupons valued at .50 each and they double, you just made $3.00 off each sheet. Later in this book I will teach you how to make additional money off printable coupons.

Newspapers:

A subscription to or purchase of newspapers for every Sunday. In the last six months, before this publication, newspapers have gone from $1.50 a paper to $2.50. Does that really matter? No, because you get much more than $2.50 worth of coupons from the Sunday paper.

File Folders:

File folders will be used to file the coupon inserts from the Sunday paper. Once you get the paper, take a marker and write the date on the outside of each insert, then put them in the file folder. That's it. There is no cutting, clipping or sorting until you are ready to make your list. If for some reason you did not mark one of the insert, look where the insert bends, there you will find the date of the publication. Then file it away. Here is an example of my file folder systems:

1st folder-Miscellaneous. This is a good folder for pullies or tear pads.

2nd folder-Printables. If I have printed coupons offline it will go here.

3rd folder P&G (Proctor & Gamble). Proctor & Gamble has a separate folder because it only comes out once a month. When a new Proctor & Gamble publication comes out, remove the old one (if it has expired) and put in the new one.

4th folder SS 2/26 (Smart Source February 26th)

5th folder RP 2/26 (Red Plum February 26th)

And so on.

There are many different sources to find out the current deals and sales ads. Following are just a few:

Southern Savers

Coupon Mom

Grocery Shop For Free

These are all user friendly but look around to find which website works best for you. You may find yourself using multiples as they all have their own style of information. Here are a few things to keep in mind.

Each author of these websites live in different areas of the United States. What does this mean for you? They are looking at the deals in their specific area. Generally, most of the deals will be about the same, however, some will not. If you find a deal you have really been looking for, I encourage you to go online to the store and look at their flier or look at it in the Sunday paper to verify they have the same deal in your area. Nothing is worse than having everything together for a fantastic deal, getting to the store, only to find out the deal is not happening in your area. Look over their biographies. Looking over their biographies will generally tell you the area they live in. For instance, the author of Southern Savers lives in the Columbia, South Carolina area. When compiling information for the website, it is generally specific for the Columbia, South Carolina area.

Chapter Two

**The Fun In Pharmacy**

Typically, when thinking about Pharmacies such as Walgreens or CVS you are likely thinking about medications. When I think about Pharmacies, I think about making money and getting products for FREE. Yes that's right Free. Pharmacies, just like grocery stores, have sales every week. They will also have seasonal sales (covered in Chapter one).

Here is a list of items you should be able to get FREE from a pharmacy:

Shampoo (2.99)

Conditioner (2.99)

Toothbrushes (3.29)

Toothpaste (3.29)

Make-up (5.99)

Some allergies medications (seasonal) (Small box 5.99)

Pain medicines (6.99)

Stylants (2.49)

Hair care products such as scrunches and barrettes (1.99)

Mouthwash (3.99)

Deodorants (4.97)

Not only should you be able to get these products for free, if you bought the Sunday paper on the first of the month and got the Proctor & Gamble insert, the majority of these things can be money makers.

BIG PICTURE: The Sunday paper cost about $2.50. The total of the above items on a low end sale is $44.97 before taxes. If you were able to get any of the above items with just one coupon you would have already paid for your paper. If you were able to get 2 or more items (which you should be able to get at least 7 of these a month), not only will you have gotten FREE products but you will make money. Money In The Bank.

Now how do you do that? I have had the most success with CVS and Walgreens.

CVS:

CVS Pharmacy has a pretty simple coupon policy which will be cover in later chapters. CVS reward system is called Extra Care Bucks or ECB. This is used just like CVS money. Extra Care Bucks can also be used like a store coupon. In order to receive Extra Care Bucks you must sign up for a CVS card. This CVS card will allow you to get extra discounts for items in the store and there is no charge to sign up.

Extra Care Bucks are given with three different programs.

The first step in getting started with Extra Care Bucks is to sign up for their emails. Remember to give your new email address. Generally CVS will offer an incentive such as $3.00 off a $15.00 purchase or $5.00 off a $25.00 purchase, just for signing up. It will have an expiration date so when signing up be prepared to start shopping at CVS. When making the first trip to CVS for shopping, be sure to have the coupon in hand. I recommend shopping for the big items with this coupon such as Charmin (Proctor & Gamble) 16 roll toilet tissue or Bounty (Proctor &

Gamble) 8 roll pack of paper towels. These items can easily add up and coupons can be found in the first of the month papers. If caught at the right time CVS will run a deal for spending $30.00 in Proctor and Gamble listed products and you will receive $10.00 back in Extra Care Bucks. What a great way to start the savings!

The most common way to get Extra Care Bucks is with sale items. Extra Care Bucks are given on sale items once the item is purchased. For example CVS may run a deal on Colgate toothpaste for $2.99. Once the purchase of Colgate toothpaste is made, CVS will give back $2.99 in Extra Care Bucks which can be used on anything in the store except tobacco, lottery, alcohol, gift cards and the usual prohibited items. In essence this makes the product free. The fun thing CVS does is they will also allow the use of a manufactured coupon and/or store coupon on items which receive Extra Care Bucks. So if you are paying the $2.99 for the toothpaste and you have a $1.00 manufactured or store coupon then you will only pay $1.99 out of pocket. Plus CVS will still give you $2.99 back in Extra Care Bucks. What does all this mean? It means you just got free toothpaste plus $1.00 in profit, minus any taxes.

Special Note: Always remember to look at what the limit is per item. The limit may be 2 per CVS card. You can still purchase 3 of these items however you will only receive the deal on 2.

Next, sign up for CVS's Beauty Club, this is a FREE offer from CVS. Once signed up for the Beauty Club, you will receive $5.00 for every $50.00 you spend. Men this does not mean that you have to go in and purchase a lot of make-up to get this deal. The Beauty Club categories include the following:

Cosmetics

Hair Care

Skin Care

Acne Treatments

Eye Cream

Facial Moisturizers

Hand and Body Lotions

Sun Care & Outdoors

Bath

Bar Soup

Brushes and Sponges

For Children

Oil & Sprays

Body Wash & Scrubs

Bubble Bath & Salts

Hand Soap & Sanitizers

Powders

Facial Cleaners:

For Men:

Facial Cleaners

Cologne & Aftershave

Body wash & Scrubs

Facial Moisturizers

Healthy Skincare

Sensitive Skin

Supplements

Signing up for the CVS beauty club is like a double payday.

Many of these products will have a sale where you will receive

Extra Care Bucks and get credit for the Beauty Club.  To make this deal even better you will probably have a coupon for the item and Extra Care Bucks from a previous order to help pay for them.

CVS store coupons. CVS has store coupons which prints from a red kiosk located in the store. Take the CVS card, scan it at the kiosk, if you have any available coupons they will print out. These store coupons can be stacked with manufactured coupons for extra savings.

Quarterly Extra Care Rewards. :

Finally, CVS has an Extra Care Buck's program for the pharmacy. You have to sign up at the pharmacy for this program and it's free. For every 10 prescriptions you fill at CVS and they scan your card, CVS will give back $5.00 in Extra Care Bucks. If you have a 90 day prescription filled you will receive 3 credits towards the 10 required for $5.00 ECB back. Since we are scanning our cards every time we go to CVS, this makes for a fun deal because you do not have to think about it.

Walgreens:

Walgreens has several different saving programs. Like CVS, the incentive to make purchases at their store is to receive Register

Rewards (RR).  Register Rewards is like having Walgreens money and can be used on most items in the store except Tobacco, alcohol, lottery tickets, gift cards and the usual prohibited items.  Register Rewards also cannot be used on the same item you received them for.  For example, if you received $2.99 in Register Rewards for Colgate toothpaste you cannot use the $2.99 received in register rewards to purchase Colgate toothpaste.

Many times items can be found which will give you the same amount back as the purchase cost (minus tax).  Special note regarding Walgreens coupon policy: you must have the same amount of items (or more) than what you have in coupons.  For example, if you purchased Colgate toothpaste and had a $1.00 manufactured coupon and had another $2.00 off in Register Rewards, you would be using two coupons for the same items (one manufactured and one store).  This is okay however you need to find one additional item so you have two items to purchase and two coupons.  My suggestion would be to find a filler item.  Filler items are best found in the clearance section.  If you are shopping after a major holiday, look for the discounted seasonal items. Seasonal items can sometimes be found for up to 75% or even 80% off the original retail value. Locate the store's clearance items, find something for less than .25 or see if they have anything in the store for .25 or less. Cute pencils for a dime make great stocking stuffers. Finding an inexpensive item gives you two items with two coupons. I would much rather have a little something I can donate or give away and be able to use my additional coupon to save money.

Register Rewards do expire and expire quickly so it is advised to use them as quickly as possible. A good practice would be to buy an item which is receiving Register Rewards in one transaction and used the Register Rewards received in a second transaction. It is very disappointing when you are looking through your coupons and find one that has expired; it is just like throwing money away.

A great advantage of getting Walgreen's Register Rewards is the barcodes on them. They also have, in the box with the expiration date, the words Manufactured Coupon. Register Rewards come from manufacturers and act just like money. Many groceries stores will take these as part of your coupons.

Simply take one to the grocery store you typically buy from, go to customer service and ask if they accept these manufactured coupons. The customer service representative may instinctively say they do not recognize Walgreens as a competitor. This may be because they view the coupon as a competitor's coupon, at this time you should point out the words manufactured coupon. The worst they can say is no. If the answer is still no, then use it at Walgreens and nothing has been lost. If they do take them, GREAT. Next big idea: Get all items together then take the amount of Register Rewards to the meat department. This is how to cut down on meat products. Use your Register Rewards. Let's say you have received $12.00 in Register Rewards this week, then get just as close to $12.00 in meat as possible. If meats are not needed, you can always use it on the balance of the grocery bill after already using coupons, making the total even lower.

Walgreens also has a rebate system. Rebate items can be found online or in the sale ads. When rebate items go on sale, purchase them and submit for the rebate. You can purchase a rebate item using a manufactured or store coupon or both. When using a coupon, this will lower the out of pocket cost. Once the rebate has been submitted you will receive the full amount of the item minus taxes. Rebates can be submitted by mail or online. Also once the rebate has been submitted it could take 8 to 10 weeks to receive the money.

There are 3 ways to receive Walgreens rebate funds. Check: a check will be mailed to your home address on file, so make sure your information is accurate. This check can be taken to your bank and deposited. Visa prepaid debit card: The amount of the rebate will be loaded on to a visa prepaid debit card which can be used for other purchases, anywhere. The Visa prepaid debit card acts like a debit card. Finally, the rebate can be deposited into a paypal account. The amount of the rebate will be direct deposited into a paypal account listed on your account. The choice is yours to make.

Walgreens has a coupon book produced monthly. These coupons will expire around the end of the month at which time a new book will come out. These books are filled with store coupons and usually these items go on sale. When these items go on sale, look for a manufactured coupon which can be stacked with a store coupon. Keep in mind to have the same amount of items (if not more) than coupons.

Walgreen's newest program is called Balance Rewards. There is not a fee to sign up for Balance Rewards. You can sign up for this rewards program online, however, you will not receive a card. In order to receive a card you will need to go to the local store and ask an associate to link an account. If you sign up for the rewards in a store, you will receive a card at that time.

You currently do not need a Balance Reward card to receive sale prices or Registered Rewards however the only way to receive points is by using a registered Balance Reward card.

Redemption can start with as little as 5,000 points and can be used both in store and online. Points can add up quickly. Keep in mind the points you receive now cannot be used towards your current purchase but they can be used on your next purchase. Balance Reward members can also get sale priced items at Duane Reade stores.

There are many ways to earn points. Get points on featured items each week in the weekly sales ad. When looking for them in stores, search for the blue tags on store shelves. Remember items change weekly.

Walgreens offers 500 points for ever filled prescription. If Walgreen's is your pharmacy of choice, you can choose to auto-refill online to earn points on a regular basis. Currently Walgreens is promoting healthy living by promoting walking. Walgreens offers 10 points for every mile walked when you sign up for Walk with Walgreens. Simply log your steps with your linked membership and earn points. Remember to always be honest.

5,000 points = $5.00

10,000 points = $10.00

18,000 points = $20.00

30,000 points = $35.00

40,000 points = $50.00

Points can be checked online, using the Walgreens App or by checking the bottom of your receipt.

In addition to earning points through prescriptions, if you are a AARP member, link your accounts and receive exclusive benefits.

**Chapter Three**

**School and Office Supplies:**

There are many deals out there where you can get most of your schools and office supplies for next to nothing and many even free. Let's start with school supplies.

**School Supplies:**

Many teachers are supplying children with pencils, pens, paper, erasers and even book bags. How can they not? Could you let a child sit in your classroom without the ability to finish their classwork? The shame of it is many teachers do not know how to get many of these items for FREE. Instead, they send home wish lists with students asking for parents help or ask to get local donations. With these few steps, you will not only be able to supply your own children with school supplies but also help out other children who do not have the ability to get what is needed during the school year.

The best time to purchase school supplies is in the middle of summer. Stores that have the greatest discounts on school supplies start having sales 5 to 6 weeks before school begins. This is the time to stock up.

The best places to get schools supplies is either at a pharmacy such as CVS or Walgreens or in an office supply store such as Office Max or Staples.

CVS offers Extra Care Bucks for the price of school supply items. For example, CVS may have ball point pens on sale for $1.99 and they will give you $1.99 back in Extra Care Buck. If you use ECB already in your weekly routine, then you will most likely already have some ECB to start with from the prior week. When CVS has the sale on school supplies, simply use the ECB from the prior week, purchase the school supplies and receive

ECB back.  Sometimes you may need to make more than one transaction to get all the school supplies you needed.  Watch out for the quantity they limit you to.  If you go over the quantity limit you will not receive the Extra Care Bucks back, making you pay full price.

Walgreens works the same way as CVS except you receive Register Rewards instead of Extra Care Bucks.  CVS and Walgreens will take manufactures or store coupons for items they are offering 100% back on.  When this happens these items become money makers.  For example, Bic pens go on sale at CVS for .99 and CVS is offering .99 back in Extra Care Bucks.  The Sunday paper has a coupon for .50 off one pack of Bic pens and when scanning your CVS card at the red kiosk, you received a .50 off store coupon for any pen product.  When you used both the manufactured and store coupons, you will only pay the local taxes out of pocket and you will receive .99 back in Extra Care Bucks.  This is called money in the bank.

Office supply stores such as Office Max and Staples are great for those teachers who try to help out less fortunate students.  When a teacher signs up for office supply reward systems they are able to receive additional discounts and are able to purchase more than the usual quantities that are giving to the open public.

Staples:

The first stop for saving with Staples is to go to their website and register or make an account. By signing up with Staples this will allow them to send coupons in the mail. The expiration dates on mailed coupons from Staples is usually several months. The mailed coupons range anywhere from receiving free gifts with a minimum amount purchased of $30.00 to $50.00 off a $200.00 purchase. When first signing up with Staples rewards system, you may receive a coupon for 20% off your entire purchase. I know after reading different ways to get many items for free, you are probably thinking what am I going to do with just 20% off? Keep reading and you may be surprised at what 20% off will get.

Easy Rebate Form:

Staple's new advertisement with sale items are put out once a week. In the sale ad you should look for items with a 100% easy rebate. The easy rebate will give 100% back on a purchase (minus taxes). The process for submitting an easy rebate form is rather easy. Find the item and purchase it. Once you have purchased the item the cashier will print off an Easy Rebate Form. Take the form to the computer, go to www.staples.com, log in and input the information off of the Easy Rebate Form. In about 4-6 weeks you will get a check in the mail for the required item. If you are unsure of the correct item to purchase, check with an associate to assist you. The item must match in order to receive the rebate. This is not Staple money and does not have to be taken back to Staples to use. This check is like one received from an employer, you take it straight to the bank and deposit it. It is truly that easy.

Staples Rewards:

Staples reward system's name is easy to remember because it is called Staples Rewards. There is no fee to sign up and you can sign up in the store. Once signed up verify that all information is accurate online. With registration completed, make a purchase, have the cashier scan your card and you will get a credit for the purchase. When making a purchase online remember to always log in with your Staples Rewards Card number so you can get credit.

What are some of the benefits of the reward card?

5% off instantly.

$2.00 in rewards for every ink cartridge recycled.

Free Shipping on all orders.

These are just a few of the benefits. Rewards can be earned for the amount of money you spend. Now, this is where it can get tricky. I am going to show you a system where you will first spend money but then no longer have to. In doing so, you may not reach the point where you are getting extra money back simply because you are not actually spending any money out of pocket. If you are not getting money back, then that means you are doing it right.

How it works.

When making a purchase with a percentage back in Staple Rewards, this means Staples will put the amount of the reward (minus sales tax) in your Staples account. A good place to start is with paper. Staples may have a case of paper on sale for $49.99. When purchased they put $40.00 in your Staples Reward account to spend later. The initial out of pocket for the case of paper is $49.99 plus tax but wait, remember the 20% off coupon you were waiting to use until the paper went on sale. 20% off $49.99 is $10.00, so your out of pocket is now $39.99. Staples will add $40.00 into your rewards account making the case of paper FREE. Local discount stores offer a realm of paper for $4.74 or $30.97 for a case. It usually takes until the 20th of the following month to show up in your account. If you make a purchase on the 10th of April, you will not see your reward balance increase until the after the 20th of May. So don't be alarmed if you do not see the rewards in your account immediately. These amounts will expire so be sure to use them.

The fun part begins. Now you have $40.00 in your staple rewards account. Staple's is having a sale on Sharpie Pen Retractable Grip Fine Point Pen 2 per pack for $6.29 with $100% back in Staple Rewards, limit 3. Log into your Staples Rewards account, verify your rewards, and add the maximum amount of pens into your cart for a total of $18.87 (plus tax). You have $40.00 in rewards and we do not want to miss out on any additional savings. If there are other items with 100% back in rewards, add them to your cart. If there are no other rewards offered at this time, look for items you can use such as toilet tissue or coffee. Either way make sure you have at least $40.00 in your cart prior to checking out. If you do not use the full $40.00 you will lose anything left over. During check out, instead of using your debit or credit card number use your Staples Rewards. You will need to sign into your staples reward account, view your rewards. Each reward will be listed separately with their own certificate number and pin. Copy down the number and pin number you wish to use for your purchase. Go back to your cart and fill in the information. You can only use one reward at a time. You have spent nothing out of pocket and Staples is putting back 100% of the rewards items you have in your cart. You receive your package in the mail with free shipping and all is good.

How can Staples help with school supplies?

Staples is the only company I have found that annually has a penny sale. Usually they have multiple items for a penny with a limit on the amount of items you can purchase. They also require a minimum purchase to receive the items for a penny. Regardless of these terms it is still a great deal. Another offer Staples makes periodically is a free book bag with a minimum purchase.  Items that are not on sale will tend to be quite a bit higher than your normal discount store so you may feel a little frustrated trying to come up with a minimum purchase in school supplies.  So let's cut down on that frustration and don't try to come up with the minimum while purchasing school supplies. Staples also sells coffee, toilet tissue and paper towels otherwise known by Staples as break room supplies.  These items are competitively priced with other stores and Staples will accept manufactured and store coupons.

This is an example of how I would use Staples without using my Staples Reward money at school time.

The penny deal is on. With a limit of five per item you can get 10 count package of pens, 100 sheets of notebook paper, 10 count #2 pencils, pink erasers and rulers for a penny each with a minimum purchase of $25.00.  To make this deal even better Staples is offering a free book pack with this deal while supplies last.  My purchase would include the following:

1-Packs of Charmin 16ct     $10.96

2-Folgers Coffee     $15.98

5-Packs of pens     .05

| | |
|---|---|
| 5-Packs of notebook paper | .05 |
| 5-Packs of Pencils | .05 |
| 5-Packs of erasers | .05 |
| 5-Rulers | .05 |
| My total is | $27.19 |
| -20% off | $5.44 |
| -$.50 Charmin | .50 |
| -$2.00 off Folgers | $2.00 |

My new total is $19.25 out of pocket, not to mention how much the actual school supplies are worth. Keep in mind, if you have money in your Staples Reward account, it can be used towards this purchase making your out of pocket expense even lower. This is great but what's better? Did you make sure they signed you in with your Staples Reward's account? If so, you received an additional 5% (or .96) back into your account. .96 may not sound like a lot but let's say your child's teacher list includes hand sanitizer or Kleenex for their classroom. You can run to your local discount store and pay the $1.00 out of pocket or you can head down to Staples, use your rewards and pay pennies.

Office Max:

Office Max has many of the same concepts as Staples. Office Max rewards is called MaxPerks. There is no cost involved for signing up. The money in the MaxPerks account will expire. Office Max offers free shipping for orders over $50.00. Keeping their offer of free shipping in mind, it would be my suggestion when placing your first order, to purchase items with 100% back up to $50.00. Paper, as with Staples, would be a good start. I know the original $50.00 seems like a lot, however, if you think about the concept, you won't have to spend any more of your money at Office Max. You will simply roll their money over each time you make a purchase, making all your items from now on FREE.

One of the nice benefits with Office Max is for every $500.00 spent, Office Max will give you an additional $25.00 in your Maxperks account. If you have a teacher's account they will give you $10.00 for every $75.00 you spend up to $100.00 in a year's time. They have, in the past, considered home school moms as teachers. This looks great, however, if you use the system right you will never get it and that's a good thing. Once you pay the initial $50.00 (you always get free shipping when you spend $50.00 or more) you will only use their money so you will never get up to spending $500 out of pocket. You may get $500 in products but you won't actually have to spend it. If you get to a point where you just don't want to do this anymore, remember to print out your certificates and take them to your nearest Office Max, make a purchase and be done with it.

## Chapter Four

**Deal-of-the-day Sites, Appliances, Books and Movies**

**Deal-of-the-day Sites.**

Deal-of-the-day (also called flash sales or one deal a day) is an e-commerce business model in which a website offers a single product or service for sale usually for a period of 24 to 36 hours. Other offers may stay on the site until certain quantities have been purchased. Potential customers register as members of the deal-a-day websites and receive online offers and invitations by email or social networks.

These can be older companies that are trying to generate new business or new companies that are trying to get a business started. This is a good way to get your name out to the public.

They will offer the public a deeply discounted price for their products or services. The deal-of-the-day site will take a percentage off of what they originally make from their sales. Either way as a consumer it's a win win. Once the business makes the sales, they have a higher chance of having repeat customers. Those customers will tell more customers and finally their company is off and rolling. Some deal-of-the-day sites sell their own products. Most of the time, you can receive an incentive just for signing up. The incentive can be anything from money, which can be used on their site or your choice of many offered gift cards mailed to your home.

Deal-of-the-day sites are not just for large cities. Many will have national deals or items that can be purchased online from any location.

These deal-of-the-day sites are popping up all over the place and are not limited to the United States. These sites have been found in Canada, Australia, UK, Singapore and China. These are only a few:

LivingSocial

LivingSocial is the local marketplace to buy and share the best things to do in your city.

With unique and diverse offerings each day, they inspire members to discover everything from weekend excursions to one-of-a kind events and experiences to exclusive gourmet dinners to family aquarium outings and more.

They help local businesses grow by introducing them to high-quality new customers and giving merchants the tools to make new members. These new members can easily become regulars. Based in Washington, DC, they have more than 70 million members around the world.

Currently they have offers globally in the following areas:

North America – 313 Cities

Asia – 8

Europe – 52

Oceania – 40

South America -4

Below are a few examples of past Living Social daily deals.

--$50.00 carpet cleaning for up to 4 rooms

--Thrift store offering a $40.00 voucher for $20.00. (Here you can get already deeply discounted clothing for 50% off.)

--A window treatment store offering $300.00 worth of window treatment for $90.00

--Plumbing shop offering a plumbing inspection for $69, a value of $139. This would be great for anyone who is in the market to buy a house.

--A Golf Resort & Spa offering one night's stay for $129 (for two people). Now, I know you're saying that's pretty pricey. Well this will also include an appetizer ($10) at the local Tapas, $25 gift card valid for onsite restaurants, breakfast (10.00 each) for two and a $15 golf credit for two. Take all that into consideration and the room is now down to $44.01. And if you have a $10.00 credit in your Living Social account for signing up, you could also use it, making your room now $34.01. Not to shabby.

Groupon:

Launched in November 2008, Groupon features a daily deal on the best stuff to do, see, eat and buy in 48 countries and soon beyond. They have about 10,000 employees working across their

Chicago headquarters, a growing office in Palo Alto, CA and local markets throughout North America and they also have regional offices in Europe, Latin America, Asia and others around the world. Groupon has been featured on The Today Show, Good Morning America, Reuters, CBS, NBC, ABC & Fox.

Categories offered by Groupon are:

Food & Drink

Events & Activities

Beauty & Spa

Fitness

Health

Home & Auto

Shopping

Below are a few examples of past Groupon daily deals.

--Yoga classes $60 for $17

--Mexican Grill $54 for $27

--Golf Resort $199 for $99

--Hair Salon $60 for $27

--JC Penny portrait studio with sitting fee, includes prints and CD.  $125.00 for $25.00

--Picaboo Photo books $70.00 worth of products for $19.00

Zulily

Just what is Zulily?

It's a new online store offering daily sales events on top-quality apparel, gear and other goodies for moms, babies and kids. They carry the great brands at the lowest prices. Members enjoy savings of up to 90% off retail prices. Zulily loves to find deals on favorite styles and introduce their members to exciting new brands.

Why join?

It's like a ticket to an amazing sample sale. Only members can take advantage of Zulily's low prices. Membership is free and signing up is fast and easy. Once you're a member, you'll be the first to know what they've got to offer every day.

How zulily works

They are not a traditional online store. Instead, they feature new items every day. They find great buys from lots of brands and work with them to ship you the goods. They don't keep stock in a warehouse. Zulily events last 72 hours . . . then they're gone! New brands move in and get their three days on the site.

Every day they launch new limited-time shopping events. Members receive a daily email revealing the latest events. From there, members click to their site and shop. Members can also go straight to the site to shop every morning.

Every day is different, so if you're looking for something specific, check back often. You are bound to find most anything for moms, babies, and kids on Zulily!

Gilt

Have you been looking for that gift that makes him or her go WOW.  Gilt is the place for you.  Gilt is for those who love designer styles and have used my techniques to save money.

Gilt, like all of these sites, is for members only.  It is free to sign up and start saving.

Gilt provides instant insider access to today's top designer labels, at up to 60% off retail. Become a member and find something new every day for women, men, kids and home as well as exclusive local services and experiences. Sign in and see what inspires you.

First Come, First Serve

All sales take place only on www.gilt.com and their full collection of merchandise is always available at the start of the sale, so be sure to log in early.

Advance Preview

To introduce each brand, their designer bios and reels give you a preview of upcoming sales, must-have pieces and featured designers.

You can find many designer brands in categories such as:

--Women

--Men

--Baby and Kids

--Home

--Food

They have had many different designers which include Prada and Escada.

Always remember to read any fine print on deal-of-the-day sites. When receiving a voucher rather than making a direct purchase, check the expiration dates. These will expire some in a year and some in a month. So look carefully and know what you are buying.

Appliances

Whether we rent our homes and we have to supply our washer and dryer or we own our home and we need everything the appliances are something we have to have.

There are many different options when it comes to purchasing appliances. One of the most economical ways to purchase a new appliance is to find a local scratch and dent store. When I had to replace my refrigerator, the one I choose had many scratches and dents. Those scratches and dents just added a little character. We're not talking about huge gashes just little dents and scratches. The owners of these shops have a connection with big name stores. The big name stores aren't allowed to accept an item that appears to have been turned over or may appear something has happened to it. So these appliances are passed down to other options. The items are still brand new just with a few cosmetic issues.

My Frigidaire Gallery 22.6 cu ft side-by-side counter-depth stainless steel refrigerator retails for $1299 plus tax. I paid $500 because it had 3 dents on it. Two on the side that couldn't be seen and the other was a great place to put refrigerator art. Mechanically, it is as sound as the one I replaced when bought brand new at full price. It was a huge savings.

So buying an appliance with dents doesn't appeal to you. Another option is to go to a department store outlet such as Sears. KitchenAid is one of the leading high end appliances on the market. They sell anything from coffee pots, griddles, stoves and refrigerators. With the durability of these appliances comes the amazing price tag attached. It doesn't surprise me that the KitchenAid 20.9 cu. Ft. Built-In Side-By-Side Refrigerator retails for $8500.00 new or that a refurbished model will still run you close to $6000.00. I'll take new over refurbished any day but I am not willing to pay $8500.00 for it. So what can you do besides go get a lower end model? Go to a Sears Outlet. There you can find the same model for $4250.00 or half the cost. Plus what's better than money back.  Later in this book I will show how you can get an additional $85.00 back off of this purchase.

Books

If you are like I am then you love to read. I mean actually hold the book in my hand and flip the pages, really read. Get out a highlighter, if something sparks an interest or turn down the pages.  I don't really like to go to the nearest big chain book store and buy a book for $14.99 plus some.  So, what is my solution? Book clubs.  I am a fan of book clubs.

Book Club companies offer you special introductory offers on books if you commit to purchasing additional books by a certain length of time.  This time could be anywhere from 12 to 24 months.  Many people think poorly about book clubs because of the cost associated with the remaining purchase.  You have to purchase your remaining books at a specific price or higher.  Not only that, but you will have to pay shipping, so now it doesn't look as appealing.

Generally, you can receive an introductory offer of at least 4 books for about $1.00. At the time of this publication, Double Day Book Club is offering the following introductory offer: 5 books for .99 with the commitment of purchasing 4 more books within the next year.

How to make this offer work for you. Add the 4 books you want in your cart. Once added you will then be asked if you would like to purchase another book for a lower cost of approximately $5.99. Pick another book. This additional book will go towards your commitment. Now your commitment is to only purchase 3 more books. You will then be asked if you would like to purchase another (6th) book for a smaller cost than their usual club prices. Do not buy the additional book. This additional book will not go towards your commitment. You now have 5 books in your cart for a total of $6.98. The book club will then add in your shipping for about $15.69. This is kind of steep for shipping, I know, especially when they are going to send the book media mail, which is the cheapest and slowest way to ship books. I do not want you to worry about the shipping in this transaction. Your new total, with shipping is $22.67 or $3.78 per book. Not a bad price considering you can choose to get these books in hardback.

About your commitment. You are probably going to look around the site and see many books for around $17 or more and that's okay. Book clubs generally will put their books on sale in groups. You have a commitment to purchase 3 more at this point. Their group sales are 2 for $25, 3 for $33 or $4 for 40. During this time, they typically will also offer $2.49 to FREE shipping over any order of $25 or more. Since you need to purchase 3 more books, do so now. Your total is $33 and for this example we are going to say your shipping is $2.49, making your total $35.49 and you have completed your commitment. Once you receive your books cancel your membership. I know this looks like $11.83 a book and it is for this transaction alone. However, if you put the totals for all 9 books together, you would come up with $58.16. Take your total and divide it by your 9 books and you get $6.46 per books (which could all be hardback books, if you choose).

Movie Clubs

Recently, my husband and I have put thought into the future of our children and future grandchildren. We thought we would like to have good movies for them to watch, that would be age appropriate. After looking through our Disney movies, we realized, we still have them on VHS and VCR recorder to play them on. Knowing these items are becoming obsolete, I took the opportunity to go to our local stores to find out exactly how much Disney movies would cost us. After much looking I realized, I would have to pay at least $19.95, plus tax ($21.15) for a new Disney movie. Thinking this was really not in our budget I went to the internet and found the Disney Movie Club.

How do movie clubs work? They work primary the same as book clubs. They both give you introductory offers and you have a commitment to purchase more in the future. After testing out my theory with Disney Movie Club I found this to be the best place to get new movies at the best rate possible. Don't get me wrong, you can always go to flea markets or Ebay to purchase these same movies. However, when I purchase them through Disneymovieclub.com I know they are authentic and if there is a problem with it, I will simply return it with no hassle. Upon the publication of this book Disney Movie Club is offering the following. You can purchase 4 movies for $1.00 with the commitment to purchase 5 more in 24 months, at $19.95 each. Once you have picked out your four movies, you have the opportunity to purchase an additional movie for $14.95. Purchase the 5$^{th}$ movie. The 5$^{th}$ movie will go towards your commitment leaving you to only buy 4 more. With this introductory offer, Disney Movie Club gives FREE shipping. Your total will be $15.95 plus tax. For this example we will use 6% sales taxes for a total of $16.91. Once you have received your movies, purchase your additional 4 movies. Try to make your additional movie purchase all in the same transaction, to save on shipping. Your shipping is $3.49 for the first movie and $1.49 for each additional movie. They will have additional offers, the same as the book club however, typically only the first movie will count towards your commitment. If you are not interested in getting the additional offers and only having the first movie count towards your commitment, to get the best possible pricing, try to purchase all of your remaining movie commitment at one time. They must be full priced movies. I understand the cost of 4 movies at one time with shipping and taxes is going to be about $92.55.

The Big Picture. The total of all 9 movies is $109.46 or $12.16 each. If you go to the store and purchase these movies at $21.15 you would have spent $190.35. Your savings is $80.89 or $8.99 a movie.

Now you are done. I had a difficult time finding where to cancel my commitment. Go to your FQA (Facts, Question and Answer) page. There are multiple places on this page you can either call or send an email.

Special Note: Chapter 5 is also going to show you how to save even more.


Chapter 5

How to make money in 20 minutes a month.

One thing that is going to help you either save additional money or even make money is to keep  receipts. The easiest way I have found is to get 5 folders and label them with your two favorite

Pharmacies, your two favorite grocery stores and one for other.
For example:

Folder One: CVS

Folder Two:  Walgreens

Folder Three:  BiLo

Folder Four:  Publix

Folder Five:  Other

These folders are for rebates.  Rebates pop up periodically and there is no rhyme or reason for them.  However, when I come across a rebate offer I want to make sure I have the receipt.  Generally, companies which offer rebates will ask for proof that you actually bought the item.  Proof may come in the form of the original receipt, barcode or both.  The best way I have found to do rebates is to look for them while shopping.  Items with rebates have a little sticker on the product saying something to the effect of "Try me for Free".  Remove the sticker (rebate) and read the requirements.  Many times the requirements include purchasing the item, then mailing the receipt and the barcode to a specific location.  If this is an item you would like to try, then purchase it and send off for the rebate.  Once you receive a rebate check (which can be deposited into your bank account) you have only paid for the stamp to mail the rebate in and the item was free. In cases you may have paid for the taxes on the item as well.

The Sunday paper is another way to find rebates. Once you have pulled the inserts from the Sunday paper, flip through them. Sometimes the inserts will have rebates for items. Simply read the instructions, make the purchase and send off for the rebate.

Southern Saver's is a good place to look for rebates. The writer doesn't actually have a datebase for rebates but she will give you a link when one matches up.

Here is an example of a money maker rebate deal that is happening as of the date of this publication. Neosporin has a new product out. This product comes with 3 Neosporin parts and is great for traveling. It has a body wash for sensitive skin, a eczema cream and eczema anti-itch cream. I purchased this one at Walgreens for $12.99. There was a$2.00 off coupon which brought my total down to $10.99 plus tax. So here's the good part about rebates and coupons. There was a rebate which gives back the full price (minus taxes) up to $15.00. I spent $11.65 for this product, out of pocket and .46 for a stamp. The rebate company (Neosporin) paid me $12.99. I got the product for free and they gave me an additional .88.

The check you receive will be an actually check. You will take this directly to your bank and deposit or cash it, just like any other check.

Another type of rebate is when a company will give you a gift card in place of an actual check. At the time of publication you can receive a gift card rebate for Theraflu. This is how it worked for me. Wal-Mart has Theraflu for $4.97 plus tax. There was a coupon in the Smart Source insert of the Sunday paper for $2.00 off. So with tax you are paying $3.15 for this product plus .46 for the stamp for a total of $3.60. But you will get a gift card for $5.00. Once you receive the gift card for $5.00 you are making $1.40 to buy this product.

There are many ways you can earn gift cards and cash on the internet. After looking through a bunch of them, I have chosen to use the following six. These six are sites I use and have received either a check or gift card from.

Swagbucks

Mypoints

Inbox Dollars

Ebates

Shop At Home

Upromise

The most important thing to remember about these sites is to fill out your profile. This is how each company gets the information to send you different ways to receive points or cash. They usually also give you either points or money to fill it out. Think about it like this, if your profile is not filled out how will companies know where to send your money or gift certificate to. These sites have a lot in common, however, I use each of them differently. Usually these sites give you small amounts of money or points to use towards something on their site. You earn points by reading emails, taking surveys, watching videos, using search engines, or buying things you would normally buy. The surveys can be lengthy and with little pay and because of this I do not take the time to do them.

This is what I have found works best for me, on each site.

# SWAGBUCKS

Swagbucks is a website with a points earning system. The way I earn my points on this site is by downloading the search engine toolbar. It takes about 30 seconds. Then every time I go check for coupons, I go to my facebook account, check my email...anything, I use their search engine toolbar. They give me one point each morning I log in and as I continue doing things on the web throughout the day, I just type it in their search bar. They will periodically give me points and add it to my account. That's it. They even gave me points to download the toolbar.

Every Friday is Mega Swag Bucks Day (MSBD), which means better odds of winning our BIG Swag Bucks denominations! Simply search naturally and with a little luck, you'll be winning large bills (points) starting at 20 Swag Bucks.

Additional ways you can earn Swag Bucks is by watching videos, taking surveys, shopping, completing special offers, vote in the daily polls, finding swag codes, sending in prize photos and videos or trading in books and video games.

I have taken their poll and was given 1 swag buck for doing so. You simply answer one question. After I answered the question it asked if I wanted to watch a video for 2 swag bucks, which I did. The video was 31 seconds long on Dr. Scholl's inserts. After watching the video it gave me a link to receive a $2.00 off coupon for Dr. Scholl's inserts. Technically, I earned 2 swag bucks and $2.00 for watching a 31 second video. That's pretty good however, there is no guarantee that you will get a coupon or the video is for something you are interested in. These are things you will have to decide for yourself.

The points are good for many different things. At this point I have 2682 points and I can purchase any of the following things, using my points:

1 Yr subscription to Golf Weekly – 45 issues for 2399 pts

1 Yr subscription to Martha Stewart Living – 12 issues for 1999 pts

Gifts

Candles

Board Games (Sorry, Life)

Baby Toys

Jewelry

Movies (Toy Story 3 or Iron Man 2)

Pacer Fans- Game Issue Warm-up Shirt


Gift Cards

The following gift cards can be purchased with points ranging from 1055 to 1275 points.  Each gift card is worth $10.00

Overstock.com

Lowes

CVS

Starbucks

Home depot

Domino's Pizza

Kmart

JCP

Sears

The Gap

Old Navy

Regal

Papa John's

Bass Pro Shop

Steak & Shake

Barnes & Nobles

A lot of these will come in the form of a e-gift card which means it will come straight to your email account on file. They can either be printed out and taken to the store it is for or you can use the codes on lines.

Example of how I would use it.

I have enough to get 2 $10.00 Old Navy Cards. Old Navy is having their Super Cash Sale right now. What that means is for every $20.00 you spend, Old Navy will give you back $10.00 in Old Navy money, up to $30.00. Since this is spring, I will purchase $60.00 worth of winter items (which should be on sale for at least 50% off). That's actually a minimum $120.00 worth of clothing. I would use my $20.00 gift cards making my out of pocket $40.00 (a 66% savings). On top of that, Old Navy will give you $30.00 in Old Navy money to come back and spend again.

MYPOINTS

Mypoints is exactly as it sounds-another point system.

Ways you can earn points through Mypoints:

Surveys

Read emails

Book travel

Play games

Search the web

Print coupons

I do not use their search engine because they usually give you about 75 points a month. Swagbucks pays more through their system. However, Mypoints will send emails. All you have to do is click on the email and they will generally give you 5 points. I will get anywhere between 10-15 emails a week, so I am getting 50-75 points weekly alone on just emails. That is anywhere between 200 to 300 points a month. 150 points is about $1.00 in their system. Not a lot of excitement there but there's more. Another thing I like about Mypoints is they will send you emails that will ask you to register for things such as diabetics.com. They may give you 125 points just to register. Registering is simply giving them your email which you use for spam and sometimes your name. What does registering do? The diabetic website will send you emails. Remember to sign up with your new email (Chapter One). Mypoints will also give you different offers. Such as:

Netflix. Netflix is just over 8.00 a month. However Mypoints may send you an email to sign up for Netflix. This is not going to be a 5 point email. Mypoints will give you many points for signing up. This is what I did. I received the email, set up an account, they gave me the first month for free and 2000 points into my Mypoints account, which is about $13.00, or enough to get a $10.00 gift card. Typically you will have to pay for one month to receive credit. After making the first payment of $8.47 for the second month, you will receive the 2000 points worth $13.00. That's a profit of $4.53

Points can add up quick. At this time I have 4599 points in my account. I can choose from any of these $25.00 gift cards.

- **HSN** 3,700 Points

- **T.G.I. Friday's®** 3,700 Points

- **T.J. Maxx** 3,700 Points

- **Landry's Restaurants** 3,700 Points

- **Cracker Barrel** 3,700 Points

- **Papa John's** 3,700 Points

- **Kohl's** 3,700 Points

- **Baja Fresh** 3,700 Points

- **P.F. Chang's** 3,700 Points

- **Sears** 3,700 Points

- **Applebee's** 3,700 Points

- **Starbucks** 3,700 Points

- **Regal Entertainment Group** 3,700 Points

- **California Pizza Kitchen** 3,700 Points

- **Steak `n Shake** 3,700 Points

- **Pizza Hut** 3,700 Points

- **Jack in the Box** 3,700 Points

- **Claim Jumper Restaurants** 3,700 Points

- **Rainforest Cafe** 3,700 Points

- **Kmart** 3,700 Points

- **Red Robin** 3,700 Points

- **West Elm** 3,650 Points

- **Panera Bread** 3,650 Points

- **Red Lobster-Olive Garden** 3,650 Points

- **Barnes & Noble Booksellers** 3,650 Points

- **Old Navy** 3,650 Points

- **REI.com** 3,650 Points

- **Groupon** 3,650 Points

- **Pottery Barn** 3,650 Points

- **Overstock** 3,650 Points

- **Saks Fifth Avenue** 3,650 Points

- **Chili's-On The Border-Maggiano's - Romano's Macaroni Grill** 3,650 Points

- **Williams-Sonoma** 3,650 Points

- **Pottery Barn Kids** 3,650 Points

- **Motherhood Maternity** 3,650 Points

- **Bass Pro Shops** 3,650 Points

- **Staples** 3,650 Points

- **The Limited** 3,550 Points

- **Finish Line** 3,550 Points

- **Shutterfly** 3,550 Points

- **Foot Locker** 3,500 Points

- **L.L.Bean** 3,450 Points

- **Macy*s** 3,450 Points

- **The Children's Place** 3,450 Points

- **NutriSystem** 3,450 Points

- **Omaha Steaks** 3,450 Points

- **Banana Republic** 3,450 Points

- **Bath & Body Works** 3,450 Points

- **SpaFinder** 3,450 Points

- **Magazines.com** 3,450 Points

- **Bloomingdales** 3,450 Points

- **Gap** 3,450 Points

- **Express** 3,450 Points

- **Boston Market** 3,450 Points

- **FTD** 2,700 Points

There are currently 205 rewards offered.

Most of the gift cards are not electronic gift cards given to you through your email but they will be actual gift cards mailed to your home address. Those that are e-gift cards will be listed as e-gift card and will be emailed to you.

You can also print coupons and earn points. Earning 10 points for every coupon you print and redeem. These coupons are printed from coupons.com. If you regularly use coupons.com now would be the time to print your coupons through Mypoints and receive points for your printed and redeemed coupons. Be on the lookout, Mypoints will periodically give you double points for printing and redeeming coupons as well as give you bonus points for redeeming a specific number in a month's time.
Find your favorites, shop at your grocery store, and save money while you earn Points. Plus, earn 25 Bonus Points when you print and redeem 10 or more Coupons.com, Smartsource.com,

Coupon Network or Hopster coupons or when you save and redeem any 10 or more Cellfire coupons in a month.

Share and Earn up to 1,000 Points

Earn up to 1,000 Points when your friends print and redeem coupons.*

When your friends print and redeem:

50 coupons you earn 100 Points

250 coupons you earn 500 Points

500 coupons you earn 1,000 Points

Although you can earn points for printing coupons which you will already be doing, this is not the website I recommend printing them from.

Inbox Dollars:

I really like inbox dollars because they pay you actual money. It's a check that you take straight to your bank.

They let you cash out after you have earned $30.00. The down side is they charge you a $3.00 processing fee but when you cash out, they will put an additional $3.00 into your account.

What you are about to hear is not going to thrill you, just yet. Just remember, if it's not worth my time, I'm not going to tell you about it.

How this works is they will also send you emails. All you have to do is click on them and they will put .02 into your account. We know this is not a lot of money so don't dwell on it. Okay so we have clicked on their .02 emails. There is a little trick. When you click on the pink tab button it will open a new page. You will find another pink button to click on. You must click on that second button to get credit. Still not a lot of money right?

How to make it easy. So now you have all these emails that you have to weed through in order to get to the ones that are going to pay you. This works best with a Yahoo account. Simply open up your email account and at the top of your messages you will see; From, Subject and Date. Most email accounts are set up to view the most recent in dates. Click on the Subject tab and it will sort your emails in alphabetical order. So all your MYPOINTS and INBOX DOLLARS will be grouped together. Just start at the top of each section and clicking on the emails. I do this every Friday and it takes me about 5 to 7 minutes to complete. On average 20 minutes a month for both sites. That's an average of 3600 points (on the simple 5pt emails without registering with anything for additional points) or $25 on this site alone. That's $12.50 a hour. This may not seem like a lot, but you are barely doing anything for it, plus, this is only one of the sites.

Think about the Netflix that paid you $8.00 and only took 5 minutes of your time. That's $1.60 a minute.

Special Note: The more of your profile you have filled in, the more emails you will receive.

Another simple task you can do is watching videos. You will find this on your home page about in the middle. It's called "Easy Cash". Once you get there, in the middle of the page you will see the following:

Videos:

Search & Earn (this is a search bar). I don't do searches here because I get paid more with Swagbucks however, I want you to download the toolbar. It takes about a minute and they will add around a $1.00 to your account.

Share & Earn-This is giving your opinion and is very time consuming with little payment.

Do & Earn – These are research task and they are difficult to do not knowing exactly what they are looking for. They may have you research for a particular bed and breakfast in Scotland and want you to find the exact address which will be a foreign address. I've tried these and for the time it takes for me find exactly what they are looking for, and only earn from .08-.32 is not worth my time.

Videos do not pay a whole lot but if you aren't doing anything else you may want to sit down and watch a commercial which is what the videos are. You can earn a little extra that will take you to the $30.00 cash out level. This is how they work. You can do 3-5 a day for .04 to .05 each, depending on what is available on that day. They are usually a minute or less. Most of mine are about 30 seconds long. One thing you have to remember about the videos is you have to watch them. There typically will be a 2 digit code which will roll either on the sides of the video or the top or bottom. After the video ends you have to put in the 2 digit code to get credit. Don't worry, if you looked away and missed it, there will be a button to restart the video, to give you another opportunity.

Now to the fun part. Remember those books clubs I was talking about. This is one of the websites I go through to get the books. Right now these are the book deals they have with memberships.

Double Day – 5 for .99

Children's Book Club – 6 for $2.00 plus you get a free gift

Book of the Month Club – 4 for $1.00

Now, here's the exciting part. Inbox dollars will give you $10.00 for signing up with these book clubs. So you are getting discounted books plus $10.00 back.

Remember the section on Book Clubs, (Chapter Four). Our total for 9 books was $55.67 or $6.19 per book. When you use Inbox Dollars and they put $10.00 into your account, just for going through their website, your books now cost $45.67 for 9 books or $5.07 each.

Another thing I like to get from Inbox Dollars is Ink. When purchasing ink through Inbox Dollars they typically will give you money back. They have a website called Double Ink and is currently offering $7.00 back simply by going through their website to make the purchase. Double Ink is a company that does supplies ink. They are compatible ink cartilages. I have used these for a long time and have only had an issue with two of them. You're probably thinking with the price of ink two ink cartilages are pretty expensive. Rest assured, when I contacted the company they sent out 2 new cartridges at no additional cost. Let me show you how to save with these ink cartridges. I have a Kodak printer. When researching the best prices, I went to Walmart. I can purchase the combo pack for $32.97 (plus tax). I can purchase the color ink ($19.97 plus tax) and black ink ($12.97 plus tax) for the same amount of printable pages. If you look at this carefully, you will see that it is .03 cheaper to buy them individually than it is to purchase it in a combo pack. With tax I would be paying $34.92 for a black and colored ink cartridge. I admit I print a lot of stuff so I needed to find a more economical way to print.

At Double Ink, if you spend $55.00 you get FREE SHIPPING. They have a set of 3 black cartridge and 2 colors for 34.99. If you purchase 2 or more, you get an additional 10% off. This is tax and all. With the 10% off it brings your total down to

$62.98. Plus you get $7.00 back into my Inbox Dollar account, which brings your total down to $55.98 or $5.60 for each ink cartridge .

EBATES:

Ebates is a rebate system. They also pay cash. You will get a check in the mail that you take directly to your bank. It is very easy to use. You simply sign up. Once you are ready to shop online, simple go to their toolbar, located in the top right hand corner of their webpage and find the store you are looking for. Click on the link. Ebates will then tell you what percentage they are giving back on your total purchase and if they are having any special deals at your particular store. In addition, on this link if Ebates has any promotion codes currently running for the store you are shopping at, it will be listed here. Checks are only sent out quarterly but they add up. I have been a member for 2 years and have earned $206.86 for doing what I was already going to do anyway. It's called Money In The Bank.

Ebates is super fun for anyone who shops online. A lot of people shop primary around holidays. Shop at Walmart online and let Ebates pay you back.

Examples:

This is an example of what I am working on.

We really need a new Lawn Mower. I can get one at Home Depot for about $150.00. I will wait until around Memorial Day because they generally will have 10% off making my mower $135.00. I will save MYPOINTS until I get a $50.00 gift card making my mower now $85.00. I will order it online through EBATES to get 3% put into my account and have it delivered to the store so the shipping is FREE. Since gift cards act as actual money, I will have to pay the taxes on the $135.00 (8.10 in taxes) which also means I will get 3% on the total of $143.10. Ebates will put 4.92 in my account. (85.00+8.10-4.92). That makes my mower $88.18 or 41% of the original cost.

This is one way I use this system. Another way is that I simply save the gift cards and money throughout the year. I wait for Black Friday or Cyber Monday and I shop for Christmas with the cards or money I have earned all year long. No more extra credit card bills or worrying all year long how to save up for Christmas. Simply go online and cash out or choose your cards around the middle of October to the beginning of November. This will allow the checks and cards enough time to get to you. Before my Christmas shopping begins I typically cash out at the beginning of October. When they all come in I know how much I have to spend, then I start looking at the deals.

Chapter 6

**Eating Out, Movies, Entertainment & Vacations**

**Eating Out.**

With 6 children you would think we don't eat out a lot. I think we would surprise you. I believe I have come across the most economical way to save on eating out at nice restaurants. It's called Restaurant.com.

Restaurant.com is an internet site that allows you to purchase gift certificates at a discounted rate. Like most things you have to look at the print. I have not ever had any expire on me. If you are purchasing a $25.00 gift certificate, you must meet a minimum spending requirement such as $35 at the restaurant. Not to worry, you won't actually spend $35.00 on the meal out of pocket. In addition, generally you will be charged around a 18% gratitude. This gratitude is in addition to the minimum $35.00 requirement. We would always tip anyway so this is no big deal. This site is very user friendly. Simply create an account and log in. If it is your second or more times going to the website, their start page will be a search page. On the search page put in the zip code for the area you are looking for restaurants to eat at. Once it generates a query, you can login to your account at the top right hand corner of the page. Once logged in and the zip code has been put in, their system will pull up every location in the zip code area that is participating in their program. Examples of certificates you may see with discount codes applied:

| Type of | Original | Cost after | Cash | New |
|---------|----------|-----------|------|-----|

| Restaurant | Cost | coupon code | Back 15% thru Ebates | Out of Pocket Total |
|---|---|---|---|---|
| Upscale Bistro | $100.00 for $40.00 | $24.00 | $3.60 | $20.40 for $100.00 |
| TGI Fridays | $25.00 for $10.00 | $6.00 | .90 | $5.10 for $25.00 |
| Mexican | $5.00 for $2.00 | $1.20 | .18 | $1.02 for $5.00 |
| BBQ | $5.00 for $2.00 | $1.20 | .18 | $1.02 for $5.00 |
| Sushi | $25.00 for $10.00 | $6.00 | .90 | $5.10 for $25.00 |
| Greek | $25.00 for $10.00 | $6.00 | .90 | $5.10 for |

| | | | | $25.00 |
|---|---|---|---|---|
| Seafood | $75.00 for $30.00 | $18.00 | $2.70 | $27.30 for $75.00 |

Once you make the purchase, the gift certificates will go into your account.  When you are ready to use them, log back into your account, pick out the certificate you want to use, print it out, take it to the restaurant and you are ready to eat.

For instance, we love seafood.  Restaurant.com has a location on their site for Harbor Inn (a seafood restaurant).  Generally you would purchase a $25 gift certificate for $10.  Nice saving right.  Well let's keep going.  Periodically, Restaurant.com will have a promotion for anywhere from 70 to 90% off the already discounted cost of the certificate.  I usually will wait to buy mine until it is at least 80% off, so we will work with these numbers.  When purchasing my Harbor Inn gift certificate, my price starts at $10, I will use the promotion code given by Restaurant.com and it will take off 80% or $8.00 from the original $10.00 leaving my balance as $2.00.  Sounds pretty good doesn't it.  Do you remember in Chapter 4 the company called Ebates?  I will go through Ebates first and generally they will give me around 15% off my out of pocket cost and put it in my Ebates account.   I will actually pay $2.00 for my certificate and Ebates will give me .30 back, making my actual total $1.70.  I take my certificate worth $25 to the restaurant, make a $35 or more purchase plus gratitude, my bill is $41.30 minus the $25 and I pay $16.30.  Don't forget about the additional .30 added to your Ebates account.  Final cost $16.00.

Let's look at the math:

$35.00 Meal

<u>$6.30</u>            Gratitude

$41.30 Beginning Total

$25.00            Minus Gift Certificate

<u>$00.30</u>            Minus Ebates refund

$16.00 Final Total

Special Note:  You can only use one gift certificate to the same restaurant once every 30 days.  For example, if you are planning to use a gift certificate from Restaurant.com to TGI Fridays on July 19th, you will not be able to use another TGI Friday's gift certificate until August 19<sup>th</sup>. Feel free to use any other gift certificate during the month but only one gift certificate to the same restaurant once every 30 days.

Another way to save on eating out.

At the end of the year and during certain holidays, many restaurants will have promotions when purchasing gift cards. For instance Outback Steak House may offer a $20 bonus card for every $100 you spend in gift cards. Applebee's may offer a $25 bonus card for every $100 you spend. If any of the locations that offer this promotion is a location you like to eat at during the year, then this deal is for you.

The way this works, is you purchase the gift cards which can be used any time after your purchase. You will receive an additional bonus card with your purchase. The catch is you can only use the bonus card during specific dates. They are normally around the time of purchase. The bonus cards will expire so be sure to check their expiration dates when making your purchase or ask your server. The traditional gift cards purchase will not have an expiration date and can be used any time.

Big Idea. If this is a place you would already go, buy the gift cards and save the bonus card for Valentine's Day or any other upcoming special occasion, as long as it is before the expiration date. It becomes a perfect treat for that special night out. Special Note: When making a gift card purchase, the restaurant may specify that you cannot use the gift card for your current meal purchased. Read the print and if you have any questions ask your server.

Movies

Well, if it's getting close to your date night and you want a big idea, let's talk movies. Movies are getting more and more expensive. Really for the price of a movie ticket you can wait for the movie to come out in stores for a couple of months and buy it new, take it home to watch anytime you want. But what's the fun in that.

There are a few different ways to save on movies. If you are planning to actually go out to the theater, one of the cheapest ways to watch a movie is to go during Matinee times. Matinee times and pricing may vary from theater to theater. Matinee times are typically movies showing before 6:30pm but could be as early as 6pm. The trick is to catch the movie before the 6pm cut off. During matinee times the price of the movie ticket is a few dollars cheaper and you may find the theaters themselves to be less crowded.

If your local theater has a rewards system, by all means sign up for it. Usually, you will see an advertisement pinned up somewhere. If not, ask your cashier if they have this option available. You can usually sign up while you are in line by filling out a short form. Once signed up the cashier will present you with a rewards card. For every purchase (and you must present the card so they can swipe it) you will receive points which add up to free products, money off product and even free movies.

Regal Cinemas has a promotion on Tuesdays for $2.00 on a small popcorn purchase. You can choose to get a larger size for an additional $1.00 each upped size. For example, if you have this promotion the small popcorn would be $2.00, medium $3.00 and large $4.00. Now if you have a large family like I do, your best bet would be to opt to pay the additional $2.00 for a large. Why? Regal Cinemas also allows one free refill on large popcorns and large soda products. So we will pay the additional

$2.00 and buy the large soda for $5.50. Our total is $9.50 and we always get the refills. The large popcorn and large soda plus refills are $26.00 and you will only pay $9.50. That's a savings of $16.50.

Watch out: There are many times the theaters will flash "deals" such as a large popcorn and large soda for $13.00. These make you think they are a deal and make you consider buying more than you normally would. In reality they are the same price as normal. Presently Carmike Wynnsong and Regal theaters have reward programs.

Another money saving movie idea is to go through MYPOINTS.com. You will generally get an email (or look it up on their site) for the opportunity to purchase 2 movie tickets and a $10.00 gift card from the concession stand. These gift cards can also be used for or towards the purchase of movie tickets. Their offer may look something like this, 700 points or about $5.00 worth of points for making the purchase through mypoints.com. There isn't much of a savings as far as the tickets go, however, you are getting the points just for going through their site. This is how your saving transaction will look with the value of the points you may receive:

### Traditional Transaction (No Savings)

| | | |
|---|---|---|
| 2-Movie Tickets @ $10.50 each | $21.00 | |
| 1-$10.00 Gift Card | <u>$10.00</u> | |
| Traditional Total | | $31.00 |

### Savings Transaction

| | | |
|---|---|---|
| Mypoints Movie Bundle | | $28.50 |
| Mypoints points value | | <u>$ 5.00</u> |
| Savings Total | $23.50 | |

That's a savings of $7.50

To receive the maximum benefits go to an evening movie (matinee) on a Tuesday at a Regal cinema. Get a $2.00 popcorn and a soda. At the end of the day you will still have money left over on your gift card.

These are the terms of this transaction:

The Movie Pack includes:

* 2 Unrestricted Premiere Tickets

* $10 Gift Card

Features of the Regal Entertainment Movie Pack:

* No expiration

* Premiere tickets can be used for all New Movie releases.

* Premiere tickets are unrestricted; valid for all movie show times.

* Regal Entertainment Group Premiere tickets are honored at all Regal Cinemas, United Artists Theatres and Edwards Theatres nationwide.

* Premiere ticket redemption at box office counts towards points on your Regal Crown Club Card.

Please note - these are not electronic codes, these are physical gift cards that will be shipped to the address that you provide at checkout.  This outing will need to be planned once you have received your cards in the mail.

At Home Movies:

If you are not in the mood to go to the theater why not stay home and rent a movie.

The two best options are Blockbuster and Redbox kiosks.  These kiosks are located in various places.  You can go on their websites to find the closest location to you.  Blockbuster will have a blue kiosk where redbox will have a red kiosk.  Both will run you about $1.25 for a movie. Even though that is not a lot, I still like Free. If you haven't already done so, sign up with these two companies. They will give you a free movie just for signing up. They will even give you a FREE movie on your birthday. Periodically, they will send you promotion codes to get FREE movies. Redbox is really good about sending you promotion codes to your email. Be sure to read them. I tell you to read your emails because sometimes they will send you an email with the newest movies coming out and they will enclose a promotion code for .50 off one movie making it only .75. The usual code is given for the purchase of two movies. They will subtract .50 off your total making your purchase of 2 movies about $1.50 or .75 for each movie.

Southernsavers.com will sometimes post free codes.

Blockbuster's Catch. You cannot get a free movie for a new release. It has to be out for some time. So for a new release, go to Redbox first.

Redbox's Catch. Read the print. Sometimes you cannot use the promotion code online. You can reserve online, however, when you do that you will automatically be charged. So if you have a promotion code you must go to the Kiosk to use it, when stated. Regardless of how you have to use the code, it's still a good deal.

Entertainment:

I have found the Entertainment Book to be my best source of Entertainment. These books can be found in most Pharmacy's around the end of the year for the next year's publication. They are local for your area. They typically will expire around the end of November and the first initial cost $35.00. That's a little much for a book, however, not only will you get many savings opportunities in the book, but if you go online, you will find many more opportunities which include golfing, restaurants, car rentals, and much more.

Here is a list of savings in my area:

| Piccadilly | $5.00 off $20.00 purchase |
|---|---|
| Pizza Hut | B1G1 Free Medium Pizza |
| Atlanta Bread Co | BIGI Free Breakfast Entrée |
| Dunkin Donuts | $1.00 off a dozen donuts |

A&W  Free 20oz Root Beer (no purchase necessary.

Captain D's   $2.00 off any dinner or platter

**Regal Cinema** $2.00 off any full-priced Adult admission of $8.00 or above (8 of these coupons included for a $16.00 savings)

$2.00 off any size popcorn

**Skate Park** B1G1 Free admission

**AMF** B1G1 Free bowling, up to 6 people (2 coupons included)

**Golf** Free Greens

B1G1 Free up to 4 people

Free Balls

**Gyms** Free enrollment ($99.00 value)

$24.95 membership for 6 months

**American Airlines** $10.00 off any airfare purchase

**Budget Rentals** 30% off

**National Car Rentals** $15.00 to $20.00 off rental plus free weekend day (2 each included)

**Tire Kingdom** $50.00 off a set of 4 New tires

**Retail Services includes:**

**Best Buy**

**Sears**

**Target.com**

**Costco**

Dick's Sporting Goods

Gap

The Children's Place

Jo Ann Fabric

Fantastic Sam's Hair Salons

FTD

Party City

And many more

You can get these books for less than $35.00.  Go through the emails MYPOINTS.com sends out.  They will offer anywhere between 1000 and 2000 points (or $7.50 to $15.00 worth of points) for purchasing the book.  Typically there is no shipping charge.  Any of this sounding good yet?  If you are anything like me, I don't do a whole lot in the winter time.  I wait until the end of February to purchase a book.  There is still 9 good months to use the book.  By this time of year Entertainment book will offer special discounts to sale the books they have left over.  Around this time of year I can spend around $20.00 out of pocket for this book but wait, remember MYPOINTS is going to give me anywhere between $7.50 to $15.00 to purchase the book. Not such a bad deal now, is it?

One of the things I like about this book besides all the added savings is the movies tickets. In this year's publication you can buy up to 10 movies tickets for $6.75 each with a $3.95 surcharge for a total of $71.45 or $7.15 each, in my area. In my area, movie tickets go for $10.50 each for a total of $105.00 for 10. My savings is $33.55.

Remember:

Once you have received your book, go online to their website to activate your membership. The book will come with a membership card attached. Use the member ID number on your membership card to activate your account. After you have signed in you can view even more offers. You can also download the mobile app. To download the mobile app, search for ENTERTAINMENT MEMBERSHIP COUPONS in your app store or visit www.entertainment.com/mobile to learn more.

Vacations

Vacations need to be planned. Last minute vacations will turn into a very costly adventure. I recommend planning a vacation at least 6 months in advance.

One of the biggest ways I have learned to save on vacations is to go through a site which will group your travel plans. Meaning, you can purchase a flight, motel and rental car all in one place. I particularly like to use Expedia.com for my travel arrangements. They are user friendly and if I ever have an issue, they are quick to make me happy.

Expedia has many deals world-wide at discounted rates. It's easy to check on savings you get through this site. Simply put a package together and go to the different websites you would have been using separately. For example, if you are getting a package deal on the Marriott for $59 a night, check with Marriott and see what the actually rate would be for the travel dates you have choosen. I have never been disappointed.

Big Idea:

When using Expedia.com, go through Ebates to get a percentage back. Ebates will give you the percentage back after you have made your trip.

**Helpful Hints:**

~If you are planning a trip 6 months out, check Entertainment book to see if they have a publication in the area you are going to. You can see which deals they offer in the location you are traveling to. On top of that, go through MYPOINTS to see if you can get additional points for the purchase of the book. Many times my points will offer you points for each book purchased not just the first one.

~Go to Resturant.com to see if there are any available gift certificates for the area you are traveling to. On top of that, go through Ebates to get a percentage back off of the purchase of your gift certificates.

If you have to rent a car, check your MYPOINTS point balance. You may have enough points to get a gas card. The gas card can be used to fill up your rental car therefore getting some of your gas FREE.

Another way to save on vacation is your checked luggage at the airport. The majority of airlines today are charging anywhere from $25 to $35 per bag. Some will allow the first bag to be free. If this is the case, pack light. I know if you are going away for a week, you need a week of clothes. No, not really. Ladies, take your largest bag as a carry on and put a smaller additional purse in it (if you like to change them out) if not put your shoes. You are typically allowed one purse and a carry on. This large bag will count as your purse. Take your carry on as an additional small bag, as they will measure it. In your checked baggage, only put enough clothing for 3 to 4 days and make sure your hotel has a washer and dryer, not a laundry service but an actual washer and dryer. Half way through your trip, take the 2 hours to wash and dry your clothes. Typically if the hotel has a washer and dryer they will also carry laundry detergent. I have found the detergent running for about $1.00 to $1.50. Both the washer and dryer will probably cost you around a $1.00 each. So if you had two loads of laundry, you will pay about $7.00 compared to the hassle of lugging around an additional bag and the additional charge of at least $25.00. That's a savings of $18.00.

Chapter Seven

**Clothing and Personalized Gifts**

**Clothing**

Getting good quality clothing at a descent price can be rather tricky.  For second hand clothing there are many options.  Salvation Army and Good Wills are excellent choices.  These establishments have many donation centers for people who have clothing they have or their children grown out of.  People donate the items of clothing and these companies go through them, check for any defects and price them according to the quality and brands.  There are many good finds to be found in these stores at a fraction of the cost.  These stores are great for those people who want to not only save money but give back.  These companies are non-profit organization who give back to their community.  The Salvation Army is a Christian based organization so you won't find them opened on Sundays.

Note: When making a purchase from these companies always check for buttons and zippers.  We are all human and sometimes these items can be looked over.

Consignment shops are another location to find second hand clothing.  A consignment shop is a second hand store where local people take things to resell.  Usually the items people bring in are brand name and are well taken care of.  Typically you will find clothing someone purchased and has simply grown out of. People take these items to the consignment shop and the employee will give them the once over. Once they have decided to accept the item, the shop will make an agreement to sell the item for no less than a specified amount. The owner takes a percentage of the sale once the item is sold and the consignment shop owner writes a check to the original owner of the clothing that was purchased. If helping those that give back is not a concern then a consignment shop may be just what you are looking for. They are rather picky on the clothing they choose to accept from people which makes looking through them much easier.

Stores such as Plato's Closet is another second hand store that offers quality. Plato's Closet is similar to a consignment shop as far as quality goes. They are rather picky in what they accept and only accept brand new items. The difference between a store such as Plato's Closet and a consignment shop is Plato's Closet pays the original owner up front and in cash. There is no room to change your mind. You bring in items to sell, the associate goes through each item very carefully and offers you a specified amount depending on how much they can resale the item for. This works really well when you need to make a quick buck and need to get rid of items. Remember if you are unable to sell the items you can always donate them to the Salvation Army or Good Will. Shopping in these stores have benefits because they usually only accept what is in style at the time and major name brand items are only accepted. These stores sale and accept anything from clothing (jeans and shirts) to hats, purses, shoes and accessories. It's a one stop shop at a discounted price.

Note: Look close, I have found many items with original tags still attached.

There are so many options to buying new brand named clothing at a descent price. One of the best ways I have found to buy new clothing, in stores, is during the off season. Meaning when it is summer time I am buying jackets, hats, jeans, long sleeves and boots or winter clothes. When it is winter, I start making my summer purchases such as shorts and swim wear. Two things to keep in mind when doing this. One, you will not have the latest trends but they will only be one year behind. Two, timing is everything with seasonal items. You can try to find good quality swim suits in the middle of winter but it will be difficult. Typically, once the season comes to a full close the clothing is stored away. Since they are already discounted for a quick sale, the store will set them out at the beginning of the new season. They will be extremely picked over and the sizes will be limited. The prime time to purchase seasonal items is at the change of seasons. The time change for Fall may be at the end of September but the weather may start cooling off at the beginning of September. The beginning of September would be the time to start shopping for summer clothing. At this time, you can find items already discounted with many styles and sizes still in large quantities.

Shopping online for seasonal items is also a great way to save on new clothing. Although it may be harder to find the well put together outfits, the best time to shop is during the end of year holiday season. This would be the perfect time to buy t-shirts and jeans not necessarily outfits. Many companies will mark down their off season items (which will be summer since this is at the end of the year) and offer free shipping.

Example:  Aeropostale may run a deal on summer clothing at the end of the year, typically around December.  If you have not already done so, sign up for Aeropostale emails.  Signing up for their email is also good for their sister company PS Aeropostale.  The sister company, PS Aeropostale is for children's clothing.  It is quick and easy to sign up.  Go to www.aeropostale.com and find the link to sign up.  They only ask for your email address to start with.  Once you make a purchase you can fill out the main profile information which should include your mailing address for shipping purposes.  With signing up for their emails, Aeropostale sends special promotions for different percentages off and will inform you in advance of their big sales.  Some of these sales have been as much as 70% off.  You will receive the special discounts in your email and some even come in the mailbox.  These promotions codes and special discounts are very important.  Many of their t-shirts start off at around $19.99 each.  When Aeropostale puts their shirts on sale for 70% off, the new price for the same shirt is now $6.00 each.  Is this sounding good?  Well let's remember that you probably have at least a 20% off coupon.  This 20% off coupon has either came to you in the mail or in your email. This coupon should be good to use on your complete order which will include clearance and sale item. Be sure to check the wording before shopping. The 20% is taken off of your new price of $6.00. If you do have a coupon your shirt is now $4.80 for a Aeropostale t-shirt. Not a bad deal, right? Let's not forget about the shipping. Sometimes they will offer free shipping but it's not that often and there is a catch. Around this time of year they will offer free shipping for orders over $100.00. I know that's sounds like a lot but remember you would have spent this same amount for only 4 items when it is in season. If you are trying to maximize your savings and shirts are at the best prices, then you are looking at 21 shirts (if that is what you decided to get). 21 shirts are a lot but let's think about how many people you know. You now have a few for Christmas gifts, birthday gifts, and a few for next school year. These would be perfect for families with school age children. If you buy them a little bigger, you now have a few for the following school year. 21 shirts before taxes will run about $100.80 and will qualify you for free shipping. That's a savings within itself.

**Big Idea:** Go through Ebates and get an additional 3% back, making your new total $97.80. Because your out of pocket was over $100.00 you still qualify for free shipping.

**Bottom Line:** 21 shirts would have cost you over $420 (with tax) and you are getting them for less than $98. By all accounts that's a savings of $322.00.

Don't forget the example in Chapter 5 (Hint Old Navy Super Cash Sale)

**Old Navy**

Annually Old Navy has their $2.00 sale. These sales are usually in the late Spring to early Summer. Look for two different sales. One will have $2.00 tank tops and the other will have $2.00 flip flops. Beware they will have select ones on sale with a variety of others sitting out. You do not want to confuse the two. The others sitting out near the ones on sale will be at a regular price. If you are unsure which ones are on sale ask an associate. There will be a limit of the amount you can purchase. The best idea as with any other big sale is to get there early. The most common sizes and most popular colors will go first and fast.

**Personalized Gifts**

Gifts are so much fun to give especially when they are made individualized for a special person.  Getting started can be rather easy if you have saved photos on your computer.  There are several websites which gives you free printed photos just for signing up.  Once signed up the companies send out codes for additional free items.  You can do these all year long for Christmas presents at the end of the year.

Here is a list of places to start uploading your photos:

CVS.com

Walgreens.com

Shutterfly.com

Snapfish.com


CVS and Walgreens both will give around 25 free photos just for signing up under their photo department.  Keep in mind this is completely separate from signing up for their regular email promotions.   This can be found in the photo section on their website.  All you have to do, once you sign up, is upload your pictures, pick out the ones you want to have developed, add it to your cart and choose to pick it up in the store nearest you or the one you go to most frequent. When you choose to pick up the photos in the store there is not shipping charge added because you are picking them up rather than the photos being mailed to you. Generally you can pick to have them developed and printed in an hour at no additional charge. If you need something quick, fast and in a hurry this is the option for you. Periodically CVS and Walgreens will offer a free collage with a promotion code. Since you are now signed up with their photo department you should receive promotion codes in your email inbox. Simply log into your photo account, choose the pictures you want on your collage, choose your colors, any titles or wording and again, choose to pick up at the store to save on shipping.

Shutterfly and Snapfish are both online photo shops. They have an introductory offer of around 50 free photos, just for signing up. You may have to pay for shipping. Remember when signing up, to complete your profile with your mailing address. Once your photos come in, simply start making projects. Don't forget to check your inbox for promotion codes. These online photo stores also do a variety of projects such as hardcover photo books, blankets, mugs and calendars.

You can get all sorts of personalized gifts at www.vistaprint.com. They have an array of different items, from coffee mugs, to T-shirts to note pads.

The best way to get started at Vistaprint is to go through MYPOINTS.com. Usually they will offer around 300 points to make a purchase at Vistaprint. After you get to the site, sign up and go to the free items. You should find a section for both business and personal free items. Choice any one of the free items, customize it and put it in your cart. To maximize your buying power make sure to stick with the designs they present to you. If you choose a different design usually there will be a upgrade charge. The shipping is a little stiff so I would suggest getting a few of the items, to make it even out. With anything time is everything. These gifts need to be made well in advance so you can choose the standard shipping (usually 2 to 3 weeks). Standard shipping is still a little costly than other websites but with customized items made for free it is the most economical. Here comes the fun part. Once you have made your first initial purchase, you will receive many emails offering you additional free products.  Here are a list of free items I have received and their uses:

Coffee Mug (Father's Day Gift)

T-Shirts (Family Reunion)

Mouse Pads (Christmas Gifts)

Stationary (Just for fun)

Pens (Thank you gift)

Thank you cards (self-explanatory)

Small Banners (Birthday or yard sale sign)

Invitations (Birthday Party)

Business Cards (Thank you notes)

Calendars (Christmas or Mother's day gifts)

I usually will group a few of these things together and end up paying $10.00 to $15.00 on shipping.  The shipping divided by the number of items will make for a $3.00 great personalized gift.

## Chapter Eight

Cars, Insurance, Utilities, Dentist, Hospitals and Prescriptions

Cars.

It seems on every one's bucket list is to own a brand new, no mileage, mint condition new car. Not me, I know the value of a new car drops dramatically once you drive it off the lot. We are not talking a $1000.00 drop in value rather being upside down from the moment you are in a contract. If you want something newer than a "Buy Here Pay Here" lot go to the large dealership.

One of the best ways to save on a newer car is by buying a program car. A program car is a car that have been driving around for about a year and traded in on the next year's new car or may have been owned by someone already as a lease and they have turned it in. Typically they are going to have a little higher mileage than the normal 15,000 a year drivable miles and that's okay. Do you usually drive way over that 15,000 a year? I don't. What does this mean for the next driver? If you are making this purchase to keep, it means you purchase a one year old car at a deep discount, you drive it normally and throughout the next several years the mileage evens out and so will the resale value. Not only that, I am going to get it at a huge discounted rate because of the miles. I bought my first program car at $10,000 less than the current year's car and it was only a year old. It had 30K miles on it and lasted me 7 years before I decided to trade it in. By the time I traded it in the miles had evened out making the trade in value more than expected. Speaking of trading in your current vehicle. This is another way to find a good used (nearly new) car on a large dealership's car lot. For example, if you are at a dealership which sales Dodge brands, look for a Chevy, Ford, or Kia...anything but a Dodge. The dealerships, typically do not like their competition to sit on their lots for others to see. They will gladly take the competition as a trade in but they move them off their lot as quickly as possible.

When it comes to financing, the dealers will ask you which is more important to you, the amount of time it takes you to pay it off, the amount of the vehicle or the interest rate. Do everything possible not to give them an answer. You want to be able to find the vehicle you want and talk them down on the price. Do your homework.

-Know the car you want and the value of it. In knowing the value you will need to know what the specific car you are looking for is worth at different increments of mileage.

-Know the value with different interest rates so you know in advance what the payments will be.

-Write the information down and be sure to carry it with you. Before you go in, already have in mind the terms you are willing to go with and don't be afraid to walk away. Walking away is a clear indication that you are serious about what you want. More often than not, they will go back to the table to make the sale. Remember they work off commission. If they cannot make you happy, someone will.

Let's be fair. They still need to make a living. If you are a cash customer you have a lot of leverage because the dealer will be unable to get additional money from financing. However, they still need to make money. If the car is worth $10,000 and they are willing to sell it to you for $10,500, buy the car (if it's everything you want). The sales person will still get a commission.

So you aren't set on getting a newer car and you are still a cash customer. How about a good reliable car from someone in the newspaper? Of course when looking for these cars, keep your eyes open for Or Best Offer (OBO). These sellers are willing to go lower on the price listed. Typically, they have listed the vehicle a little higher anticipating someone to haggle with them. Again do your homework. Know the value of the car you are interested in before you call the seller. If you are interested in a specific car and the seller has "Or Best Offer" in their ad, ask them in advance if they will accept the fair value of the car. Since you have already done your homework, you will know what the fair value is. If the seller is not willing to go down on the price to match what is fair, don't waste your gas to look at it. Another option to purchasing a good used vehicle is to look for a seller who has a vehicle with a salvage title. Vehicles with salvage titles have been in some sort of accident or maybe in an area where a flood has occurred. There are several different reasons why an insurance company may choose to give a owner a savage title rather than pay for the repairs. If the vehicle was in an accident and the estimates to have the vehicle repaired is more than the fair value of the vehicle. This doesn't mean the vehicle can't be repaired. Usually an insurance estimate is going to be higher than it would actually cost to get it repaired if you were a cash customer. Regardless of the situation the insurance company has processed a claim and rather than taking possession of the vehicle they have decided to pay a specific amount and give the owner a salvage title, letting the owner keep the vehicle. If you have decided to look for vehicles with salvage titles make sure you know a good mechanic and do not be afraid to take one with you. Just because someone has a salvage title and has received some sort of payment from the insurance company, does not mean they had the vehicle repairs back to the best possible condition. Keep in mind also when it's time for you to sell the vehicle, you will also have a salvage title and will need to advertise this. The benefits of this is when you list you have a salvage title, you will also be able to verify how long you have driven it without any issue and also be able to provide any service records to help ease the new buyer's mind.

Insurance

There are not a lot of ways to save on insurance but there are some tips that you should know.

Car insurance.

Usually when we get our first insurance policy we ask our parents who they have their policy with and off we go to their agent. The agent writes the policy, we think nothing about the charges, we put our down payment in the agent's hands and we are all set. This isn't always the best way to get insurance. The internet is a wealth of information. Many times you can compare insurance quotes online without having to feel uncomfortable telling someone you have chosen not to get insurance with them.

So you are seasoned driver. The first question you should ask yourself is "How long have I been with my current insurance company? " If you answered more than 2 years then it's time to shop around. Many times we get in a rut and figure, if it isn't broken don't fix it. This isn't necessarily true when it comes to insurance. Insurance companies are in competition with all other insurance companies. Many insurance agents work off commission and will work hard to get you as a customer or keep you as one.   There are many ways to lower options or deductibles to make the payments more comfortable. Remember these policies are not set in stone and can be changed to fit your needs, if your situation changes.

Teenage driver.

Most of the time, teenage drivers are still practicing and do not drive as much as an adult driver.  If this is the case in your household, list them on your insurance policy as an occasional driver.  I know as my children are getting into the ages of driving, it is mandatory to put them on my insurance, however, they do not drive a lot because they are learning.  This constitutes an occasional driver.

List your teenager on the safest vehicle you own, only.  This will keep their portion of the insurance lower than if you listed them on all vehicles in the household.  High school grades are very important for getting college scholarships but they are just as important for getting a discount on car insurance.  Check for a good student driver's discount with your insurance company. Typically you will need a transcript from your child's current school to get the discount. Schools are used to this and can provide this form.

Does your child school offer a driver's safety course or a driver's education class? If so, ask your insurance agent if they offer a discount for these. Many times you will need to provide a completed certificate or proof of a passing grade to get the discount.

No teenagers on your insurance policy? I have something for you also. Ask your insurance provider if they have a discount for bundling multiple policies such as car, home, motorcycle, renter's or life insurance. Before asking, shop around and know the different cost of each type of insurance. Once you have priced them, add them together and then call your car insurance company. If they are able to beat your research, then bundle your policies. If they are unable to beat separate pricing policies, check with other insurance companies and see what they can offer you.

Special Notes: Some Insurance companies may have the right, if you inquire about adding an individual to your policy to add that individual to your policy. This does not mean that they will but they do have the right.  Try getting an online quote before picking up the phone.


Homeowner's insurance:
Some companies reserve the right to cancel a policy for several reasons.  This can stand true for inquires as well.  Meaning, they may also reserve the right to cancel a policy for to many inquiries.  Some companies treat an inquiry the same as a claim even if they did not have to pay out for a claim.  One of the main reasons insurance companies reserve this right is because they feel that there has been additional repairs on the home or repairs are needed and haven't been taken care of.  If a minor repair hasn't been taken care of then this could lead to a much bigger, costly repair down the road.  Typically, this is when the insurance will receive a claim and in turn they will have to pay out to have this major problem repaired.  This is the insurance company's way of protecting their investments.  So think before you call.


Utilities

Electric and Heat.  Believe it or not turning your thermostat to 78 degrees in the summer and 68 degrees in the winter does help save on your electric bill.  Doing this not only keeps your AC and heating unit from constantly running and running up your electric bill it also keeps it from working as hard.  When the unit is not constantly running or working hard it will last longer.

Light bulbs.  Replacing traditional incandescent light bulbs with halogen bulbs can cut down on your utilities by as much as $7.00 a bulb per year.  Let's imagine you have a minimum of 15 bulbs through your home.  That's an annual savings of $105.00.  While incandescent bulbs can be used on dimmer switches, an important feature for many homeowners, halogen bulbs are smaller and brighter.  Halogen bulbs are also up to four times more efficient than incandescent bulbs, meaning that you can enjoy the same amount of light at a fraction of the price.  According to Energy Star, in addition to having a longer lifespan, halogen bulbs also are considered more efficient than incandescent bulbs.

In the home, switching to halogen bulbs may not only produce better lighting results, but may help homeowners save money while doing their part to protect the environment.

According to the California Energy Commission, lighting accounts for 25 percent of our utility costs in the home. By decreasing these costs, we can make a significant impact on our utility bills. Let's take a look at how trading our old incandescent bulbs for halogen bulbs can help us save money.

We'll start with a standard 100-watt incandescent bulb. If the lamp is used for 12 hours a day, 365 days per year, it will be lit for 4,380 hours each year. In the United States, homeowners pay an average of $.1099 for each kilowatt hour of electricity used [source: Energy Information Association]. In our example, the cost to run this lamp can be computed as 100 watts/1000 kilowatts x 4,380 hours x $.1099 = $48.14 per year.

Compare this to the cost for a halogen bulb. As we discussed earlier, halogen bulbs produce more lumens (lighting power) per watt, and thus, a 75-watt halogen bulb would be equally as bright as our 100-watt incandescent. Therefore, the annual cost of a halogen bulb under the same scenario would equate to 75 watts/1000 kilowatts x 4,380 hours x $.1099 = $36.10 [source: Rocky Mountain Institute].

Simply looking at operating costs, halogen lights can save us $12.04 per bulb each year when compared to traditional incandescent bulbs. Of course, we must also take into account upfront cost and replacement rates. In 2009, the average cost of an incandescent bulb was $1.00, and it had a life expectancy of 1,000 hours. Halogen bulbs, on the other hand, cost around $5.00 [source: Rocky Mountain Institute] and are expected to last 3,000 hours on average. Using our example above, we would need to spend $5 on five incandescent bulbs, or $10 on two halogens to get us through our 4,380 hours of lighting needs.

Using these numbers, our total cost for buying bulbs and paying utility bills for lighting would amount to $53.14 per year for each incandescent bulb in the home, or $46.10 using halogen bulbs, which equals a savings of $7.04 per year. At the same time, we'd use about 25 percent less electricity and throw about 30 fewer bulbs into landfills.

Many utilities companies will even provide the bulbs as well as have them delivered. Look at your local utility company's website or call and see if they have this program available in your area.

Cable.  Is Cable where you like to put your money?  Is it that one fun thing you enjoy?  If you really like having many different channels or if not but would like to try them for a while, check with your local cable company.  Most of the time, cable companies will have an introductory offer which may include your cable, phone and internet for one low price.  It is good anywhere from 6 to 12 months.  Although this offer may be good for up to 12 months you may be asked to lock into a 2 year contract.  This is a great way to get started but what happens after that introductory offer?  Your bill goes sky high.

Big Idea.  On or right before your anniversary of the ending of your promotion, call the cable company and ask them if they have another promotion running at the time.  Sometimes you will get a quick yes and sometimes you will get the standard no.  When you get the no, ask them if they are aware of the current promotion ran by DirecTV.  They are probably going to tell you no.  Tell them about the current promotion and tell them you do like them as your cable company so that is why you are giving them the opportunity to remain your provider. If your customer service representative tells you that they are not authorized to make those deals, ask them to put someone on the phone that is, such as their supervisor.

If cable is not something big in your life but you would still like to have it and for some reason the answer is just no, ask them for the lowest package available. They will probable give you a package with at least 70 channels. Tell them you want the basic basic package. It consists of about 17 channels and is around $10 a month. If you like to watch TV more than this, add Netflix for about an additional $8.00 a month. Netflix is a service that makes available online flat rate DVD's and Blu-ray disc rental-by-mail and video streaming in the United States. Established in 1997 and headquartered in Los Gatos, California, it has assembled a collection of 100,000 titles and approximately 10 million subscribers.

Having built its reputation on convenient movie rentals by mail, Netflix now offers something even more convenient: Internet video streaming. The service, called "Watch instantly" allows customers instant access to a huge selection of movies online.

There are now multiple methods on how you can watch movies from Netflix on your TV at home. You can buy a special router; use a gaming console if you have one; or even connect your computer to your TV monitor directly. Let's don't forget, Netflix also has many cable series available to watch at your convenience. Below is a list of some of the top television series available to watch on Netflix:

How I meet your mother

Angel

Fringe

Torchwood

Family Guy

Sons Of Anarchy

Scrubs

Futurama

The Wonder Years

Fraiser

30 Rock

The Walking Dead

Doctor Who

Star Trek: The Next Generation

Twin Peaks

The West Wing

Parks And Recreation

The X Files

Sherlock

Friday Night Lights

Firefly

Madmen

Freaks and Geeks

Buffy the Vampire Slayer

Cheers

Lost

The Office

Arrest Development

For about $18.00 a month you can have cable and many many movies.

Dentist, Hospitals and Doctors

There's several different reasons why we have these types of bills and many of them are unavoidable.  Let's focus on the ones that can be affordable.

Dentist.  So it's time for your routine cleaning and the dentist has found other issues which need to be addressed.  Here are your two options:  1)  don't have the work done or 2) plan to have the work done.  So now we are planning.  Many insurance programs will pay up to about 50% of dentist claims.  Your dentist tell you your insurance company  is going to pay all but $200.  Check with your dentist and see if they have the following program in place.

You pay the full amount which is $400 and you file the paperwork with your insurance company yourself, if they give you a 10% discount on the total cost.  Your beginning out of pocket expense is $360,  the insurance company reimburses you their portion which should be about $180 to $200.  Once the insurance company pays you, your final out of pocket expense went from a definite $200 to somewhere between $160 to $180.  It may not sound like much but really how many times have  you or a family member gone into the dentist office and had additional expenses. At the end of the day or year it all adds up. Hospitals and Doctor bills. They are infamous for large bills and there isn't really a whole lot we can do about it. Usually our insurance is going to cover a good portion of the bill, but what about the remaining. As much as we would like to get that bill taken care of, the hospitals would like to get it off their book, especially by their fiscal year. The fiscal year can vary from hospital to hospital. You can make small payments until their fiscal year gets close. When it does, many hospitals will offer anywhere from 25% to 50% off of your balance if you can pay it in full. They have gotten the majority if not all of the money they need from the insurance company now, they just want it off the books. Pay them the difference and you will receive a paid in full letter.

Word of caution: Keep all the bills you are sent from the hospital or doctor's office. Match them with benefit paperwork your insurance company sends you. This benefits paperwork will provide information as to how much your insurance company has paid to the claim. This is very important. If the doctor or hospital has not placed a claim, then you will be charged the full amount. You will not know this unless you are matching up your paperwork. I personally have received an in-house collection notice for close to a $1000 for a bill I never received nor was it filed with my insurance company. Our first instinct was to pay the bill and make all right with the world. After looking through and discovering the hospital had dropped the ball and never filed a claim with our insurance we made the phone call to remind them to do this. At the same time we reminded them to take us out of collections as this was by no means our fault. At the end of the day our portion of the bill was closer to $180. That would have been almost a $800 mistake and would have taken a lot of money out of the bank.

What if you don't have medical insurance and you need an antibiotic. Check with your local pharmacy and see if they have a Minute Clinic. Prices may vary, however, usually there is one up front cost and then the cost of medication. The upfront cost are far less than they traditional doctor's visit. Usually an appointment isn't required. So it's fast and easy.

Prescriptions:

Let's face it, unless you are on top of your game, lots of people need prescription and they cost money.

One of the most cost effective ways to save on prescriptions is to order them in 90 supplies from a mail ordering company such as Medco. Companies like Medco will fill a 90 supply of prescriptions at a 60 supply cost. Always ask your physician if they will prescribe at least a 90 day supply for a medication used long term.

If the prescription you are receiving is for something temporary such as an antibiotic ask the doctor of samples. Typically the doctor's office will have a sample closet. These are usually brought in by a vendor to give to patients to see how they work. The vendor is hoping for good results. If the doctor receives enough good feedback they will typically start prescribing this form of medication.

Unfortunately there are many people who do not have medical insurance and do not have any type of insurance to cover prescriptions. If you have found yourself in this situation and have a long term prescription look into getting a discount prescription card. Many doctor's office, minute clinics, and pharmacies offer discount prescription cards.  You can also find them easily online.  This discount card has no cost to them and can save you at least 10% or more depending on what medication you need.  If you find one online, simply follow the instruction and print a copy to take to the pharmacy.  The discount will be taken off at the register.

Big Idea:  If you are looking for a discount card online be sure to search Mypoints or Inbox Dollars for any incentives.

Pharmacies have a great wealth of information.  Usually there is a window to ask the pharmacist a question.  Describe your symptoms and see what they recommend.  You may be able to find a remedy in the store rather than in the doctor's office.  This would be less costly all the way around.

Drug stores:

Periodically, CVS and Walgreens will offer rewards for moving your current prescriptions from the pharmacy you are using now to theirs.  The wording on these advertisements can be a little tricky but the concept is not.  The advertisement is saying if you move your current prescription to their pharmacy they will give you XYZ.  The wording sounds as if you need to have a new prescription but this is for your current prescription. So if you currently have a prescription for high blood pressure and it is currently being filled monthly at Costco then when you move your prescription to CVS or Walgreens, they will give you an incentive for that move. These incentives can range anywhere from $15 to $25 a transferred prescription. Many will have a limit such as up to 4. If you take many prescriptions, keep this in mind. Whichever way it goes, it's free money.

Big Idea: If you do have more than the allotted limit and there are multiple pharmacies offering incentives, try taking some to one pharmacy and others to a second pharmacy. Maximize your benefits.

## Chapter Nine

### Housing (Purchasing)

So are you ready to purchase a home or already have one. This is the chapter for you.

Owning a home comes with more than just the mortgage however the mortgage is the largest part of the bill if you have made the purchase the traditional way.

A typical mortgage loan may include the mortgage payment, taxes, PMI rate and homeowner's insurance. In some cases you can negotiate the homeowner's insurance. The mortgage company will have a usual insurance company, that they already work with to obtain the homeowner's insurance. This company is working for the lender and where the objective is the same (to provide you with insurance) you may be able to find the same coverage at a lower rate, if you show around for your own insurance. Of course the main objective to paying your mortgage is to own a home but at what cost. Setting the whole "owning a home" aside, the main object to this mortgage is to pay down the principal amount as soon as possible to avoid paying as little interest as possible and to avoid PMI.

PMI is for private mortgage insurance. It can cost you anywhere between $50 and $200 a month, depending on the balance of the your loan and the PMI rate.

PMI is for the lender. The lender is requiring you to pay the premiums for an insurance policy that partially reimburses them should you default on your mortgage. I am not talking about defaulting on a mortgage such as missing a payment, I am referring to going into foreclosure. Since foreclosed homes are often sold at a "discount" then the lender will want a buffer of at least 20%. In other words, they want to be reasonably sure they can recoup the money they loaned you if the home has to be sold at a lower price than the original sales price.

However, this doesn't mean that the lenders are willing to write loans when you put down less than 20%. They just charge you more for the privilege via PMI. In this way, you get a mortgage, and they minimize their risk in offering you a loan. Private mortgage insurance is an actual insurance policy issued by an insurance company that benefits the lender. If your home goes into foreclosure and the lender is not able to recoup the outstanding balance by selling the home, the insurance company that issued your PMI will pay the lender the difference.

PMI is called "private" because it is only offered to private companies and not government agencies or public mortgage lenders. Public programs, such as FHA and VA mortgage programs, have their own mortgage insurance, but it is run differently and managed internally. However, one notable difference between PMI and mortgage insurance attached to many FHA and VA loans is that the latter never expires. In other words, you will continue paying mortgage insurance on FHA and VA loans even after your loan to value ratio has dropped below 80%.

Loan to Value (LTV) Ratio

The loan to value (LTV) ratio is what the leader looks at to determine whether or not you need to pay PMI, and when you can stop paying it. To calculate this ratio, take the amount of the loan and compare it to the current value of your house. For example, if your mortgage is $150,000 and your home is currently worth $200,000, your loan to value ratio is 75%.

When you buy a new home, your lender will look at the amount of your down payment compared to the sales price to determine your loan to value ratio. So if you purchase a home for $200,000 and put $20,000 down, your loan to value ratio is 90%.

Typically, if your loan to value ratio is more than 80%, you will be required to pay PMI.

Who Needs Private Mortgage Insurance?

Generally, if your LTV ratio is less than 80%, you are in the clear. However, if you have poor credit or are otherwise considered a high risk to the lender, you may be required to carry PMI even if you have 70%, 60%, or even 50% loan to value ratio.

You may be considered "high-risk" if you have sold multiple homes recently, have been foreclosed upon, or if you have an unsteady or undocumented income. However, this should be clearly laid out in your loan documents, and if you aren't sure how it works, get a clear answer from your loan officer before signing.

How to Avoid Paying Private Mortgage Insurance

The best way to avoid paying PMI is to not have it on the loan to begin with! If you are purchasing a new home and you will not have a significant down payment, ask your loan officer for suggestions on avoiding PMI.

In the past, a popular option was the 80-10-10 or piggyback mortgage, which used to a combination of a second mortgage or home equity loan and your down payment to reduce the loan to value ratio of the primary mortgage. This may still be available through some lenders today. But if you already in a mortgage that has PMI, you have two options to remove it:

## 1. Meet the Loan to Value Ratio

If your loan is near the 80% threshold or whatever threshold your lender stipulated in the initial mortgage paperwork, PMI will automatically be removed by the lender. In practice, most lenders wait until 78%, but if you call and ask, they may remove it sooner. But you must call and ask.

Since your lender will calculate LTV off the original purchase price, you will need to keep track of your home's current market value. In other words, if your home has increased in value, you can obtain a professional appraisal and present this to the lender as proof that the value has increased.

While professional appraisals usually cost a few hundred dollars, this can be money well spent if it gets you out of paying PMI several months or years earlier than you otherwise would have. Think about it like this. If you are on the lower end of paying PMI of $50.00 a month, that's $600.00 a year for let's say the next ten years. In ten years you will have paid a minimum of $6000.00 of money you will never get back. If your home has increased enough in value to clear you of paying PMI and the appraisal was $400.00, you have just saved $5600.00.

Already living in a home with a mortgage.

Consider refinancing to a shorter term. Before talking to a lender do your research. Search the internet for a free mortgage calculator. Bankrate.com has a complete calculator that gives you many options to choose from. Simply put in your current mortgage information such as the original cost, how many months until it is paid in full (typically 360 months or 30 years) and your current interest rate. Once you have all the information in, the system will generate a amortization table complete with your monthly payments and it will tell you how much interest you will pay at the end of the loan.

For example, if you have purchased a home for $100,000 at 6% for a 30 years loan, your payments will be $599.55 a month. $599.55 is cheaper than rent (in most areas) and at first glance seems to be a pretty good deal. The truth to the matter though is at the end of the 30 years your payments of $599.55 will total $215, 838.00. The interest paid on your $100,000.00 home is $115, 838.00. The interest alone is more than the value of your home. So are you asking how to cut down on the cost of literally buying two homes and only receiving one home?  There are several different ways to cut this cost down.

-Make additional payments once a year

-Make an extra $1000.00 (for our example but you can make any additional payments) for principal only payments.

-Make bi-weekly payments

-Shorten the length of the loan

Make an additional payment once a year.  In this example, your additional payment of $599.55.  If you are saving up to make the additional payment monthly, you will need to save $49.96 a month.  You can make the additional $599.55 once a year two different ways.  The first option is to use the payment as a true additional payment.  This will not only help cut down on interest but it will also help you stay ahead of the game just in case of an emergency arises.  The second way to use this payment is for principal only.  When writing out this check, in the "for" section of your check, write "for principal only".  This entitles the full amount of the check to go to the principal of your home and not towards any of the interest.  The goal is to get the principal paid off as quickly as possible.  Follow up.  Check your statement and verify the full amount has gone to the principal and no interest was taken off. Simply making the additional $599.55 yearly payment (without making it a "for principal only" payment) cuts your interest by $23,641.00 and it knocks 5 years and 3 months off the length of time to make the payments.

For Principal Only:

Now you have all this new "Money In The Bank" because you have been saving and are wondering what to do with it. Make a "For Principal Only" payment. Before doing this (and during negotiating the terms of the mortgage contract) verify the lender will accept for principal only payments. Typically a lender will not have a problem with this as long as you are current on your payments. If the lender does have an issue with this, find another lender. For this example we will use $1000.00 additional for principal only payments yearly. If you are saving during the year to make this payment, it comes to $83.33 a month. Again, be sure to write "For Principal Only" in the "for" section on your check and verify the amount went straight to the principal and not towards the interest. If any of the amounts you sent in went to the interest, call the company and have them change it to reflect the full amount coming off the principal. Making an additional $1000.00 yearly for principal only payment on a 30 year loan will not only shorten the length of the loan to 22 years and 4 months but it will also cut your interest down to $81,634 of the original loan. That's a savings of $34, 204.00.

Make bi-weekly payments:

This can be done anytime during a mortgage payment plan however the best time to start is at the beginning. You must be prepared to start off doing this from the beginning to maximize the benefits. So prepare yourself financially by having the first mortgage payment ready prior to the start of the loan. For example, say your first mortgage payment is due on November 1st, in the amount of $599.55. Half of $599.55 is $299.78. Make the first payment of $299.78 on October 1st and a second payment of $299.78 on October 15th (two weeks later). Your first payment will be paid in full two weeks prior to the actual due date and the interest will be calculated from the payment received date and not the payment due date. In turn, this will cut down on your interest.

Fun Fact:

When making monthly payments, you make 12 payments a year. When making bi-weekly payments you are making 13 payments a year. There are 52 weeks a year, divided by 2 (the bi-weekly equation) give you 26 payments. It only takes 2 bi-weekly payments to make a fully payment so when you divided the 26 by 2, we are giving the lenders 13 payments a year and giving them a double whammy with cutting down on interest.

Example of interest saved making bi-weekly payments:

30 year mortgage-New Interest paid $90,196-Savings of $25,642

20 year mortgage-New Interest paid $60,190-Savings of $55,648

15 year mortgage-New Interest paid $44,663-Savings of $71,175

10 year mortgage-New Interest paid $29,269-Savings of $86,569

Finally the no thought way of saving on interest. Shorten the length of your loan.

Go to any search engine (where you can receive points, previous chapters) search for an amortization table. I personally like bankrate.com because it gives many options to choose from. Input your current interest rate with fewer years until you get to a point where the payments are comfortable. If you already own your home you will have to pay a refinance fee however in the long run, the interest will be cut down and you will own more of your home quicker. If you are in the market to purchase a home simply put in the information given to you by your mortgage lender to come up with a comfortable payment. The mortgage lender will typically give the payment plan reflecting a 30 year loan. This will give the lender more interest and it benefits them. Go to the calculator, put in the interest rate, original amount of loan and any other information to come up with a number that works best for you.

Example of saving when shortening the length of your loan using our prior information: All numbers are rounded to the nearest dollar.

| Length of Loan | Interest Rate | Monthly Payments | Interest Paid | Savings |
|---|---|---|---|---|
| 30 | 6% | $600.00 | $115,838.00 | $0.00 |
| 20 | 6% | $716.00 | $71,943.00 | $43,895.00 |
| 15 | 6% | $844.00 | $51,894.00 | $63,944.00 |
| 10 | 6% | $1110.00 | $33,224.00 | $82,614.00 |

**Big Idea:**

Who said you could not use all of these examples. You very well could shorten the length of the loan to 10 years and make bi-weekly payments. In doing so, it will shorten the length of your loan and cut your interest down even further.

Let's face it the primary objective is to save money. We all need it and we all could use it, so let's exhaust every honorable avenue to accomplish this goal.

www.ingramcontent.com/pod-product-compliance
Lightning Source LLC
Chambersburg PA
CBHW060931040426

42445CB00011B/881